Dear Phillip,

An interesting read for students perhaps. Always apparent what I learned at Simmon & how good the College was to me and my family.

Gave it a few good plugs in here.

Best Wishes & thanks

[signature]

DANCING
AT THE
FOUNTAIN

DANCING
AT THE
FOUNTAIN

IN CONVERSATION WITH
WORLD-LEADING HOTELIERS

Conor Kenny

Published by OAK TREE PRESS
Cork, Ireland
www.oaktreepress.com / www.SuccessStore.com

© 2016 Conor Kenny

A catalogue record of this book is available from the British Library.

ISBN 978 1 78119 208 5

Printed and bound in Great Britain by
TJ International Ltd, Padstow, Cornwall

CONTENTS

Openor: Assot mgr which Cos (13)

(132)

asset
mgt
(135)

"Openings" re careers (144) (169)

Theline (147) and other

SPA (154)

AirBnB (157)

always Say Yes$

EXTERNAL CAREER
(168) (169) Relationships (23)

ACKNOWLEDGEMENTS

Behind every book there's a story and behind every story, a person. This is a book about people and it wouldn't have happened without the extraordinary help of a few good men and women.

My gratitude goes out to:

- The seven hoteliers, who trusted me enough to share their story and themselves;
- My own team, who allowed me the freedom to hop, skip and jump until we were done: Grace Gallagher, Patrick Redmond, Linda Halpin and Geraldine Patten;
- Mark Kenny and Jonathan Neilan, for their ideas and expert view on the cover design and key messages;
- David Clarke of Dublin City University, for challenging every word;
- Ken Coleman, for his inspirational ideas on design;
- My cousin, Gerry Kenny, master book binder, for beautiful, handmade copies of this book;
- Brian O'Kane of Oak Tree Press, for his unrelenting pursuit of perfection and sheer hard work.

McDonald's Story, Lean, best around joy
attention to detail <u>(67)</u>

CaBoeuf Service Trends Ideas

Natalie Seiler Hayes

Michael Dawn Harper
Bernard Murphy E/LM Suite (102)
Greg Liddell West Business

<u>CI7</u> 79 Importance Driven

<u>MP</u> (54) (NB) Team (129) 134 "Esprit Maps" (124)
HR (67) Empowerment/Staff U. (85)
(86)
(65) Induction Training

<u>EXTRAORDINARY</u>
9/11
Riots Paris 1998

What is a C___ ase c___en (69) (177)
Your _place_ w customer. (75) 6/. (53)
Revenright
Culture

DEDICATION 110/111

Keep it Simple (131)

For my family,
and for hotel professionals the world over.

Branding (41), (38) Albert (182) (43) Merchant (149) (54)
allegiance +(41)
Standing out very difficult (42) (100) (119)
emotion (42) (51) EMPATHY (180) (182) urgent
Teel (45) Teal)) (45) (67) (155) (183)
Client Guest (46)
house lean (52)
Sales (55) (56) (56) Sales Force
Product Brand of Point (57)
Cultural awareness (57) (78)
Strategy (58)
Leadership (187) (192) (61) (133) (133½) 135Fm(r)
EI
Complicated (64) (64)
Structure + People
Stability 134

- Management Practise: MP
- Commercial Approach: CA
- Marketing in the International Hotel Industry: MKT
- Human Resources in the International Hotel Industry HR
- The Accomodation Business ACC
- The Food and Beverage Business FB

QUAL!: QUALITY
SVCE!: SERVICE (38) (34) (8) (38) (39) FPLx (12)
(42) LIMITS?? (46) Flag (124) (128) (141)
(185)
MISTAKES: (22) Queen Furniture
(23) Golf green

OPPS OPORTUNITY (24) (102) (104)

Ideas (25) Freedom of Experience (48) Brady
Future (40) Time!! Stress Henri 155
(less) (54) (88)
PERSONAL
attn to Detail (471) Travel (88) (44) (52) (67)
K misc Conon (52) Start at the bottom (52)
(12) Continuing Education (54) Realistic
(171) career progression (63) entitlement!!!
LISTEN (37) Positive!! (66) (100) integrity (66)
Attitude (38) (61) (157) (56) (47)
Hard work 39 In Jordan (37). Wood (39) (66) (13) (126) (145)
• 110% x (114) never burn a relationship (30) Banks (130)
wip D. Parra 39 In Jordan 39. Difficult to
know but (41)

INTRODUCTION

Success seems to be connected with action. Successful people keep moving. They make mistakes, but they don't quit.
Conrad Hilton

The purpose of this book is threefold. First, it is for hoteliers who want to learn from the best. Second, it is for those thinking of becoming hoteliers and finally, it is for those who are curious about the men and women who run some of the world's finest hotels.

It is the first time, ever, that a book like this has been written.

Each conversation took place in the hotel run by the hotelier and lasted around three hours. Every hotelier was asked the same series of questions and has seen their chapter in advance. They made few, if any, changes. These are their words, their way.

The hoteliers here run, and have run, the some of best-known hotels in the world – from the Far East, across Europe and to the West Coast of America and from the Hotel Burj Al Arab in Dubai to The Savoy, London and The Waldorf Astoria, Beverly Hills. They have greeted the most famous faces on earth, hosted kings, queens and presidents and provided for the needs of the most powerful people on the planet.

Their stories are remarkable, funny, inspiring and, most of all, human. They have witnessed the extremes of humanity from 9/11 to riots and from excess to poverty.

Every story and every journey to the top has been entirely different. There is no right way. There are some constants, but it would dilute the book to cluster their stories into a scientific analysis. It is up to the reader to glean the lessons they can relate to.

As well as being high-achieving and world-leading hoteliers, it is obvious that these hoteliers are also charismatic leaders. But it's interesting that none of them used that word or saw themselves as charismatic, preferring to anchor their own high achievement in a sense of 'here to serve'.

Nonetheless, the hoteliers are charismatic; they have to be. They must combine the confidence to meet heads of state with the discipline to trawl through dull backroom essentials. They must lead, but must remain in the background. They must master a multitude of skills from service to finance, design to architecture and food to bedrooms, strategy to technology. On top of all that, they must motivate their troops daily and cope with the inevitability of human error, collapsing plans, changing circumstances and global events. These leading hoteliers have done all that and more. They are at the very top of their chosen Everest and that, in itself, is why they are special people worth listening to.

For me, it has been a wonderful journey where I have had access and the trust of the best of the best. As well as that, I have had the joy of building new relationships and learning from the world's finest, not to mention visiting the most luxurious hotels along the way. It has been fun, interesting and at times, mesmerising. Then again, hotels have always interested me, let me tell you why.

❖

I was lucky to have a childhood where my mother and father understood the educational value of travel and of family, also recurring themes in each hotelier's story. From an early age, I was travelling and it was always an adventure.

I must have been around seven or eight years old. My Dad, my brother, Dermot, and I were off to Derry in Northern Ireland. Business had taken us there.

Mus At that age, staying in a hotel was very exciting. Lifts were a playground and the endless corridors were a real-life maze. Naturally, to the distress of sleeping guests, we ran everywhere, impatient to discover what lay beyond. Eventually, exhaustion and hunger forced us back to our third-floor perch. Together in the small twin-bedded room, separated by the obligatory mahogany bedside locker, we wondered how to drain the last of our adrenalin? Dad was immersed in meetings elsewhere. We had to do something.

In those days, telephones were like priceless Ming china; you daren't touch them. But hunger and a sense of adventure were potent and intoxicating chemicals for two young boys. We stared at the huge white ceramic telephone and tested our little fingers into the big rhythmic dial. Imagining electric shocks, we'd beat a retreat only to summon up the courage and go again. Eventually, we lifted the phone, giggling nervously, our little hearts racing.

To our astonishment, a voice boomed down the line, "Can I help you?". We looked at one another, mouths open, lost for words. But, it was an opportunity, an adventure. We'd gone this far. "Can we have two chicken sandwiches please?" Now we were in such deep water nothing else mattered. "Anything else?" came the anonymous voice. Our horizons had already been stretched, "Could we have two Coca Colas as well, please?".

We lay on our beds exhausted from the stress of it all. What had we done? What trouble awaited us? We concluded we were doomed.

A loud confident knock came from the door. We froze. Nervously, four young eyes peered through the gap in the door at the man in the white jacket, his gleaming trolley matching his brilliant white smile. Theatrically, he wheeled in the finest trolley we had ever seen. He even called us "Mr. Kenny". With ceremony and style, he poured the drinks and uncovered the chicken sandwiches from the polished dishes. We were hypnotised. He left and we fell in to the role of two dandies enjoying their supper.

Still laughing at our crime, reality started to bite. Who would pay for this? No money had changed hands. Oh my, we were in big trouble.

Just then, with the remnants of the delicious treats still visible, Dad came to the door. Before him, his two young sons sat surrounded by white linen, fine cutlery, crystal glass and uneaten crusts. He paused, took it all in and burst out laughing. Confused, we laughed too – and then both of us got sick. Our first step into hotels had been all too much.

The men and women who run hotels are truly amazing. They are at the front line of emotions and egos, as well as running a business. Unlike many predictable industries, 24 hours in any hotel sees substantial change. That change must be managed and responded to instantly. Some years ago, I wrote this to explain its unique characteristics.

MP   A hotel is like a theatre. Every night when the lights go down, the show is over – another day is done. The next day, no matter what has gone before it, the show will have a new audience, often a first-time audience, and today's show must, at the very least, be better than the day before. The actors who will deliver the show are your people. If

MP   you do not motivate them, inspire them and invest in them, you will have an average show and average is not the same as memorable. After all, what is the point of a beautiful comfortable cosy theatre with great sets, great seats and great lighting if the guys on stage have no idea what they are doing? The beautiful posters will soon be

MP   poisoned by the critics' pen. The hotelier's job is to keep the actors acting and the audience smiling. It's that simple.

Every time you enjoy the serenity, space, comfort and service of a great hotel, think of the gifted artist, brilliant surgeon, professional sportsperson or enigmatic musician. In common with great hoteliers, they rarely seek the limelight or praise. Instead, they get on with it quietly; they make it look easy. After all, isn't that the art and craft of all successful people, including these high-achieving hoteliers?

Conor Kenny
Dublin, Ireland

KIARAN MACDONALD

The Savoy Hotel, London

The Tara Hotel, London
The Royal Garden Hotel, London
The Metropole Hotel, Birmingham
The Fairmont Scottsdale Princess, Arizona
The Fairmont Waterfront, Vancouver
The Savoy Hotel, London

MP I believe that success lies in surrounding myself with people who are better than me.

I don't come from a family of hoteliers. I had no family link to the hospitality business at all. My late father was a civil engineer and my mother was a dietician. I come from an Irish background: North and South, Presbyterian and Catholic. That's how I ended up being born and brought up in England, in those troubled days when that sort of marriage was frowned upon.

As I went through school, it became clear to one and all that I was never going to be an academic success. I think it came from a good place in terms of trying to inspire and reassure me, but I remember my mother saying one day, "Kiaran, I don't care what you do in life as long as you feel happy and fulfilled". And I thought, "That sounds good", just before she asked the question, "What would you like to do?". With a backdrop of hating school in academic terms – I loved it otherwise – I said, "I'd like to be a farmer, but I could never afford a farm so let's put that out. I'd like to be maybe a carpenter or an electrician, because I like doing things with my hands". My mother nearly fell off her chair in horror that despite all of her, and my father's, investment in my upbringing and education I would not aspire to something greater, so that kind of put the brakes on that notion straightaway.

I then remember sitting outside with a career book and going from A to Z because I had no idea. I feel for youngsters today, my own children included. There's an expectation that you know what you're going to do in life but you're still enjoying being a child, being an adolescent. I remember being in the same boat then. I went through the book very quickly – and came to hotelier. I didn't have any notion of what that was because we'd never really been around hotels in terms of vacations but one of my mother's close friends was the late departed Owen Dillon, who was a renowned hotelier, and she gave me her sense of what the hotel business could be about. It included travel: I liked the idea of travel. At that time, I think the furthest we had travelled to was Normandy or to Ireland – but the idea of going international was fantastic! Cooking – well, my mother was a great cook and I loved cooking at that time. So the whole notion of the glamour of hotels and me being top of the tree in terms of managing one – although I didn't know how to manage myself, let alone a business – the boxes started ticking themselves. It was a light bulb moment!

Very shortly afterwards, my mother and I went up to London to meet Owen Dillon at The Tara Hotel. I have wonderful memories of that meeting, because he spoke to me on a level one-to-one. He recalled his own background and where he came from and I was thinking, "Wow, how did you do that?". He advised that, if I aspired to be a general manager, either I should go straight into the business and work my way up or, as he recommended, I should get some academic qualifications.

So I went to Ealing College, which today is the University of West London. I wasn't going to do A-levels and so this was a way of doing a diploma and then a degree, which was what I ended up doing over four years. It was a great course, because it was heavily practical in orientation in the first couple of years. It gave me a taste of some of the technical aspects of the business in a discipline that I enjoyed anyway because it involved working with my hands and academically it was pitched at a level that helped me to grow in confidence and knowledge. I finished with a degree – and did some industrial placements during it.

When I graduated, Owen Dillon offered me my first job in The Tara. I started off in 1982 in what was then called Conferences & Banqueting – and then moved across to Reception. All the time, I was trying to figure out which was the way up to the top, realising that it was probably going to take me at least 40 years because they all seemed to be very old, these general managers!

I have been extraordinarily fortunate in the people who have helped me and mentored me in life. Three – four, if I include my father, who I always would – people have truly inspired me. Owen Dillon was one of them. The lessons he taught me were as much about me observing his style of leadership and business acumen, because when I went into the hotel business one of the reasons I was able to get in with my limited academic qualifications was that it was viewed then as being more of a *mein host* position. It was less about the business aspects in terms of the income statement and more about supporting and driving the custom coming through and bringing the hotel to a level of service delivery and reputation – all the things I had worked on over the years at college. But at The Tara, Owen was way ahead of his time because he approached everything from a business standpoint and he analysed aspects of business in a way that was never talked about and certainly had no visibility whatsoever at college. I learnt so much from him. He lived and breathed being a people person: he had a tremendous amount of both character and interest about him as a person and you could see him using that in interactions with both colleagues and customers.

I cut my teeth in The Tara. Then I moved on to The Metropole Hotel in Birmingham, a big hotel, with a big conference business, and moved from there back into London. There was then, and I think it exists today to an extent, a status associated with hoteling in London – a perception that managing a hotel in London provides you with some sort of unique positioning and skills that those who are out in the provinces don't have, which makes it very difficult to come back into London. I think it's an absolute load of rubbish, always have and always will! But it was absolutely something that, when I was in Birmingham, I got a sense of. The Metropole was a good move for me at the time but I certainly found evidence of that negative perception when I started applying to move back into London.

Anyway, I came back into The Royal Garden Hotel in London. I was fortunate enough to be appointed Food & Beverage Manager, working for another famous hotelier, James Brown. James would forgive me for saying that he was a very tough General Manager and that he worked to build that reputation. Again, through some level of adversity in terms of business experience, he taught me a lot – sometimes in unusual ways.

I have always been the kind of person who wants to be the bird that gets the worm, so I'd always try and to get to work ahead of anybody else. Over time, I have found that it has enhanced my overall productivity and success – in the early morning, you get time for thinking without the distractions of phone calls and the like. James was also an early bird. One morning, he called me to his office – which was never a good thing – before I had had my first cup of coffee and said, "Mr. MacDonald, what time did you come in?". I said, "Around 6 o'clock, Mr. Brown. I drove into the car park". "So you drove into the car park. And what did you see?" I thought to myself, "I barely saw what was in front of me, let alone anything specific", but I said, "Nothing really". He replied, "Go back down and retrace your steps". Now this was bizarre. It was *attention to detail.*

MP

6.30 in the morning, and I was retracing my steps down a circular driveway into the underground car park. As I went along, I saw bits of trash on the kerb – not a great deal, just little bits – but I was thinking, "It must be something far more than that. Maybe there's a big crack, a structural fault, that I should have noticed". Anyway I picked up the trash and I went back up to James Brown's office, feeling very ill at ease going back saying, "I saw nothing but this". James said, "Exactly. That's exactly what you were meant to see. You know, Mr. MacDonald, parking at this hotel is a privilege. Never take it as a given. And you are always on duty". I left his office fit to be tied. I was spitting nails for I don't know how many hours afterwards, because I thought it was a terrible way to communicate. But many years later, I'm still recounting that story. The lesson learnt? Never ever walk past anything without having a sense of attention to detail. That incident was a catalyst for me, a jigsaw piece that helped me into the person that I am today.

MP ab

After The Royal Garden, I went back up to The Metropole, to run the food and beverage operation, which was a big operation so, from a career progression, it made a lot of sense even though I was again leaving London. However, I wanted to go abroad and Rank Hotels – the owners of The Royal Garden – didn't have any properties abroad. Going up to Birmingham, I felt that their sister-company, Princess Hotels, was potentially going to offer me that opportunity. I went up there and, fortunately, was successful in that role. The Managing Director, Martin Bolland, who today is a very close friend and someone I still regard as an important mentor, had come over from managing Princess Hotels as MD of Metropole Hotels, and he facilitated me going over on an interim basis to The Southampton Princess resort in Bermuda.

MP

Like Owen Dillon, Martin was ahead of his time. He came from a non-hoteling background, which was meaningful in the context of how he approached the management of the business. One of the first things he did was to provide company cars for all hotel executives – ordinarily, general managers would have use of a hotel car but, apart from that, nobody else did. His view was that a hotel business is no different from any other business and therefore in attracting the appropriate level of talent, a company car should be a benefit that hotel executives should enjoy. He was approaching things from a much broader perspective rather than the tunnel vision of 'this is how we both run a hotel and manage our business' and so it was so rewarding working for Martin. His focus wouldn't necessarily be on things that were a priority in my life at the time – guest service delivery, etc. For him, those were a given, simply an expectation. He was focused on maximising income, on looking at capital investment and being successful – and much more so than I had experienced up to that time – in accessing significant amounts of capital to expand the business, which was done on the basis of good commercial decisions that had a back-up of good ROI and all that goes with it as we know today. Martin was always two or three hurdles ahead, saying, "Here's an opportunity for business growth and expansion" – for example, in the NEC Birmingham but also in London on the Edgware Road.

In 1995, Martin presented me with an opportunity of going to the USA as Food & Beverage Director of what was then The Scottsdale Princess, Arizona, part of the Princess Hotels group, which then was acquired by Canadian Pacific and rebranded to Fairmont Hotels & Resorts. At that stage, it was nigh on impossible to get to America because of visa restrictions, so I was extremely lucky.

I remember getting off the plane in Scottsdale. I had assumed that it would be like the Sahara desert, intermixed with cowboys, red rock and canyons, but as I was flying in all I could see was a blanket of golf courses, seemingly unrolled across the landscape. Almost before the plane touched down, I started imagining the number of days each week I'd be playing golf! I arrived on July 8, and it was 128 degrees! I knew it was going to be hot, but I had no idea until then what 128 degrees felt like – it was blistering hot! It was a very surreal experience to arrive in a climate that was so alien, in a topography that was so unique, in a functional role that, in the discipline of food and beverage, I could bring a lot to the table but in the context of Mexican and Native American cuisine, not a clue, not a clue! At that time the UK wasn't as renowned as it is today for its diversity or indeed quality of culinary offering.

In that regard I was very much a fish out of water, but my saviour was Executive Chef, Reed Groban, who in more ways than one was larger than life! One of the most passionate and creative chefs I've been privileged to work with, he provided me with tremendous support and, to some extent, protection from the General Manager who used to be the Food & Beverage Director and frankly found it hard to let go. In my view, it didn't help that he didn't have any international experience, and the thought of some Brit coming over and telling them how to run a food and beverage operation ...

It was without doubt the hardest and most stressful two years of my life. My wife, Nicky, had agreed to be uprooted, along with our then three year old son, Charles, from the family support that we had back here. I appreciate it's been done a thousand times over by other people but that doesn't make it any easier and without doubt I couldn't have done so without the support and encouragement from Nicky – then and in the years since. I'm sure that I struggled on many levels to be as successful in my role as one would like to be or one should be – so that was one aspect of added stress – and my General Manager challenged me in a fairly aggressive way every day. It's an experience that I learnt huge amounts from, and it helped to mould me as a professional, but it was an experience I would not wish on my worst enemy.

Attention to detail is, I think, a hugely important component of our business. It's probably the same for other businesses as well but focusing on ours, I think that without attention to detail you're leaving a level of vulnerability in your toolkit. So I always spend a lot of time impressing that upon on my colleagues and my team who work with me. I didn't become focused on attention to detail immediately after that incident with James Brown but it helped me to focus and taught me the importance of it.

At this level of luxury, your customer becomes very much more demanding – often very much so – but I personally embrace that, my team embrace that certainly. When you have a demanding guest, either in advance or through the experience, you very quickly get to know exactly what their expectation is. As a consequence, often a very demanding guest brings the service delivery up a level. I suspect that more often than not our execution is more exacting and more perfect for them than it is to guests who are less demanding – a sad admission, I admit. We aspire to perfection. Although we'll never achieve it, we always aspire to it. For the guest, though, it's extra fuel in the tank – you really want to do it perfectly for that guest because they have told you exactly what they want – you think, "I know what they want so I'm going to do this in this way". Unfortunately, guests don't necessarily always communicate their expectations in the right way, so it's important to nurture relationships and to help guests to turn from being aggressive and from communicating in a manner that you know is not conducive to getting the best out of your team.

MP

We had an incident a while ago now that stuck with me as a memory moment. A guest was having breakfast. It was early in the morning so there weren't many other guests there. The first I became aware of him was when he stood up from his table and started barking across the restaurant about his toast being cold. It shouldn't happen – and it was addressed immediately. But I thought to myself, "That reaction was way too over the top. I'm not connecting the dots", so I decided to go across and introduce myself and make sure everything was all right. By talking to him, I was able to find that actually his outburst had nothing to do with the toast. He'd missed his wake-up call that morning – our mistake – the toast was simply the straw that broke the camel's back. But I wouldn't have known until later about the missed wake-up call had the outburst not happened or had I not actually engaged and dug a little deeper in terms of understanding the root cause. As it was, I was able to assist in a successful recovery and ultimately a happy guest.

MP

In a cultural sense, it is so important to have this attention to detail at all colleague levels – everyone of us, from managing director to waiter, should have that sense of not just responsibility but desire. How many times have you been in a restaurant when the server comes up and says, "Did you enjoy your meal?" and you might say something like, "It was OK". But if you have left half of your food on the plate, that's a signal for the server to dig deeper. So if we don't get it right at colleague level, we miss seeing problems early enough to not let them manifest.

Culture comes from the top without a doubt, it's nurtured there – but you feed off each other. By surrounding myself with the best talent, then the culture that I as managing director believe in gets reinforced. But my own sense of culture and beliefs are constantly reinforced and modified through experiences with my team. This, despite my ever-widening age gap with my colleagues, enables me to remain open-minded to and understanding of their changing needs and expectations!

Scottsdale was a challenge for the first couple of years, but I lived through it with the strength and support of my wife, Nicky. Then we had a change of ownership to Canadian Pacific, which brought in a new corporate culture and players at senior level and even at the hotel level. That's where another important mentor of my life – John Williams – came in. John was appointed Regional VP and General Manager. One of life's true hoteliers, John could assess a P&L statement in the blink of an eye but never let any of us forget our number one priority: our guest! A man of great presence, John's quiet but exacting leadership style brought out the best in all of us, providing clear and concise direction whilst allowing each of us the independence to run our divisions. The result was we never wanted to disappoint and thus gave of our best.

After working for him for nearly a year as Hotel Manager, John turned to me one day and said, "Kiaran, how old are you?". I said, "38". "Well, it's time you started thinking about becoming a General Manager" and then he did a sly move because he said, "Have you ever been up to Vancouver?". I was now at a point where I was in love with Scottsdale as a place to live, with three young children, two of whom had been born there. We were rooted down, I was very excited with the new company and new opportunities. "No, I haven't." "You know, you should take Nicky and the family up there for the summer. It's a great place. Just have a look at it. I think you'd enjoy it." I took him at his word, that it was a great place to have a holiday. The day before I left, he said, "Kiaran, you're going up there, aren't you?". "Yes, tomorrow." "Have a look at this hotel, The Waterfront … they're looking for a General Manager and, to be honest with you, CP is a Canadian company and you've got to get your feet dirty in Canada to have a future in it. Biased I know, but if you have to live in Canada, the Pacific North West is the best place to be. So have a look when you're up there." That completely screwed up my holiday! Because I went from being relaxed to all the anxiety around the possible move.

But it was a very interesting career transition for me because I'd become comfortable and shall we say 'expert' in the world of luxury – that's the wrong word but you understand the spirit of what I'm saying – and I was now being considered for a hotel that prided itself on being a contemporary business hotel. I thought to myself, "Why would I go from this beautiful five diamond multi-faceted resort to a four star hotel? It feels like a demotion". But within one week, I went from turning it down flat to accepting it. After discussing the move with

Nicky, she said, "You've just got to bite the bullet here, Kiaran. You've got to trust the company".

It was a great experience of going from an environment where there was limitless opportunity to provide for guests – everything at Scottsdale was about the guest, everything was about aspiring for the best and the perfect in everything – into a hotel where the guests were paying less, and the facilities were not as good, but the expectations were the same: the guests expected the best experience possible in that facility.

I grew to love The Waterfront very quickly. It was as much about the people, as in my colleagues, as about anything else. Before I arrived, the hotel had a formidable reputation in the marketplace in Vancouver, which was saturated with hotels, as being such a friendly and engaging hotel – that was what it was known for. So I went into something I hadn't expected and then spent the next four years elevating it as best I could and embracing that sense of people, contribution and culture. It was a time of tremendous learning. Everybody who was there was as proud as Punch, you couldn't put them in a palace and expect them to be happier. From a guest standpoint, it was just a wonderful arena to see how they were made to feel was the most important aspect of what made up a perfect experience for them. It's stuff you talk about in training. But experiencing it helped me to develop a team here that first and foremost is built around the question: "Do you as an individual have the personality and character to be the right fit?".

Then John Williams called me to come back to Scottsdale as General Manager. I gave it a lot of thought, wondering what more could I learn and contribute by returning? However, not only had the hotel undergone significant investment but the Scottsdale resort market had expanded significantly with several large openings on our doorstep.

Having added facilities specifically to diversify the business, targeting the leisure market, I look back with great fondness on those next four years working with such a talented and driven team, supporting their creative spirit in producing unique experiences for our guests.

Fairmont Hotels & Resorts meanwhile continued to expand internationally, including the purchase of The Savoy, London, in 2005, through a joint venture. Not only was having the Fairmont 'flag' in London strategically important for the brand but also, of course, The Savoy, being one of the world's most famous hotels, brought added prominence.

Initially, the plan was to spend some £27m sterling on refurbishing the hotel but soon it became clear that significantly more capital was needed to bring this great hotel back up to its former glory and to compete once again amongst the very best hotels. John Williams, now Executive Vice President of Operations for Fairmont, championed my candidacy for the General Manager role, and so after 12 years abroad my family and I returned to the UK.

For me, there was a level of irony coming here to The Savoy, because when I graduated from Ealing College, I had applied unsuccessfully for an accelerated management training programme with The Savoy Group – but years later, here I was as GM!

I remember arriving and walking into The Savoy on my first day. At that point, I was on a mission; I had a mandate: "In all probability, we will have to close the hotel to carry out what is likely to be a £70m to £80m refurbishment in about a year's time". So my whole purpose of being was to focus on that. For me, all this was just a physical stage to do what I was set out to do. My emotional attachment here was minimal – and I remember that feeling very clearly because I had the sense that I was alien to how other people around me felt. I don't know whether it was weeks or months – more likely months – but in the months that ensued, I found two things at play: first, the realisation that The Savoy was more than the physical aspect of it – and that scared the living daylights out of me because I had no notion of what that 'more' was but I knew that it was important; and the other was how it was affecting me. It just got under my skin. I became emotionally attached to The Savoy like everybody, but in my own way. And then, as we came closer to the closure of the whole thing, the responsibility of preserving that intangible aspect and indeed bringing it back to life caused me more sleepless nights than the physical aspect where I thought, "I've got a team of people here who can surely help me and we're all putting a lot of investment in".

As we closed the front doors and raised a glass of champagne to The Savoy and the future, the front hall was full of people, colleagues and guests alike, all together. I said a few words, very emotionally charged – and then a couple of hours later, everyone was out. Everyone! For the first time in the history of the hotel, it was devoid of life. And as I walked around the hotel, only the lights were on. The heating was off because I remember feeling cold, and I got goosebumps around the enormity of the challenge. I suddenly thought, "This is all about people. What is it that everyone wants, everyone loves, about The Savoy?". And those three years of closure were for me a most beneficial time to further understand The Savoy's intangible side, its soul, and then to build that into what we have today.

❖

One of my characteristics is that I am a risk-taker. It's neither positive nor negative; it's who I am. I am a person who is action-orientated and risk-taking and an action orientation kind of go hand-in-hand. I'm comfortable with making mistakes; I don't believe in getting rid of all the mistakes before I do something, I just do it.

Fortunately, I can look back with some level of pride about my career successes – but I certainly made my share of mistakes along the way too! When I started here at The Savoy, I thought, "I have a year of running this hotel before we close the doors and I have got to make it the best it can be in that time". In the front hall was a huge mahogany concertina panel behind the reception desk. I thought, "Wouldn't it be lovely to add glass shelves and have our florist put in some displays so guests will be greeted by a lovely aroma and colour". I thought I was an absolute genius coming up with this idea – no wonder they'd put me in charge! So I got the carpenter up and told him what I wanted. I brought the florist up and told her what I wanted. Then I told our archivist. Her jaw dropped, and she said, "WHAT have you done? THAT is a bespoke piece of furniture by Viscount David Linley, Her Majesty the Queen's grandson!". And I had desecrated it by screwing holes for the shelves into it! This small incident opened my eyes to the importance of taking the time to understand each nuance of The Savoy, prior to making changes.

Another of my many *faux pas*: when I was working at The Southampton Princess resort in Bermuda with the events team, I had sold a function to a client that included having a reception before dinner out on the 18th green. Again, I was a young man who didn't know any of the nuances of what you can and cannot do on a golf course – so I got myself into hot water for allowing this beautiful green to be used in this way. But we had the reception: all the guests in black tie and long dresses in a gorgeous setting, and I was thinking, "This is fantastic. I know that, as an operations team, we've got into trouble but the client's happy". Next thing, the sprinklers went off! What made it worse, of course, was that it was reclaimed water, so it had a lovely odour! Needless to say, it did put a bit of a damper on the event – and I learnt another lesson.

I have a deep passion to help young professionals starting out in the business. For years, if you hark back to my earlier experience, there was an element of stigma about the business and there definitely was a lack of appreciation or desire to be associated with the business of serving and a lack of appreciation of the skill that goes with it, either on the culinary side or on the service delivery side – and not just in this country. I think that the way that the media has brought an appreciation and indeed an understanding of the kitchen aspect has been extraordinarily beneficial to our business, because it has opened people's eyes.

Hospitality is a significant business that has disciplines no different than any other industry: Sales & Marketing, Finance, HR, all come together and our product is both physical and also has a service aspect. Hospitality offers a huge opportunity for professional development and diversity; it offers tremendous opportunity to succeed. Promotion is not based on 'dead man's shoes' like when I was coming in and the general managers then were all elderly. You absolutely can get to the top in your 30s and 40s now. And we have a lot of headhunters poaching talent across various disciplines, into banking, into other areas – because, as an industry, we cultivate a very people-orientated and broadly-skilled talent.

I don't believe that you have to excel in all disciplines to be a successful general manager. I have a much firmer belief in having an appreciation of the disciplines, absolutely building an expertise in one or another, but surrounding yourself with talent in whom you have the belief and desire to let them grow and succeed in their own area. It just gives me a great kick to see that happen because it's not about me: it's about the end result, about the team, about the person getting the gratification of whatever they have personally achieved. I understand that my success, and the success of the business that is The Savoy Hotel, lies in surrounding myself with people who are better than me.

For The Savoys of this world, if the contact, the emotional experience, goes away, The Savoy goes away too. Because I see that being absolutely at the level of, if not higher than, the physical aspect. The beautiful guestrooms, the beds, all the rest of it are just a stage. Often they are not a differentiator. What differentiates is the experience you provide for the guest on that stage.

What will evolve in the future, I believe, will be around the re-engineering of the execution of what we do. Take something as basic as the critical path of the guest's stay: it always includes the reservation portion, the arrival portion, the stay portion and the departure portion. But this notion that we expect guests to go through a procedural step to get their key, to then do this, to then do that, to get to what they have bought in the first place, is a nonsense! We wrap it up into a pleasant arrival for you, a nice smile to make you feel at home, but we still need you to fill out this form, we still need you to sign that form and, by the way, when you go to the restaurant you can't get up and walk away to your guestroom or anywhere else until you have signed the bill. So on the one hand we are saying, "You, as a guest, are our most prized consideration, we want you to feel completely at home" – but, on the other hand, "You can't leave here, until we let you"! Somehow we have got to find ways of fulfilling our fiscal responsibility, and all that goes with it in terms of checks and balances, and at the same time give you as a guest the freedom to experience the hotel exactly how you want to experience it.

One of the most enriching aspects of working in hotels is the constant excitement that each day offers. So some memory moments to cherish. Thus far, I have two standout memories that I look back on with tremendous pride.

My first was Nicky and I welcoming Her Majesty the Queen when I was General Manager of The Waterfront in Vancouver. Her Majesty and the Duke of Edinburgh stayed with us for three days for her diamond jubilee. We were the host hotel for their stay in British Columbia. I had the privilege – thank God I didn't know about it in advance – of a private audience with them. Thanks to being so awestruck I can't remember much of the conversation but the Queen was extraordinarily gracious whilst the Duke seemed to enjoy asking me some extremely challenging questions!

My most cherished memory is when on 10-10-10, I had the enormous honour of reopening the doors to The Savoy after three years' restoration, and then on 2 November, welcoming HRH Prince Charles and our owner, HRH Prince Al-Waleed bin Talal, who officially reopened The Savoy. A glorious occasion enjoyed by hundreds of invited guests, HRHs decided, after meeting various dignitaries, to go 'off-piste' and met and conversed with many of my colleagues, showing genuine interest in each person they met. Those precious moments will likely stay with them forever, as they will with me.

PHILIPPE LEBOEUF

The Mandarin Oriental, Paris

Hôtel Concorde Lafayette, Paris
The Parker Meridien Hotel, New York
The Carlyle Hotel, New York
The Westbury Hotel, New York
Hôtel de Crillon, Paris
Rosewood Hotels & Resorts
Claridge's, London
The Mandarin Oriental, Paris

Co-author, *Service Incompris*

You can't say that you have reached
the top. You have to be willing always
to learn, and to listen.

I come from a part of France that is very like Ireland; it's really in the countryside. I was not a city boy. My parents had a little coffee shop – pub is a better word – based around sports. My father was one of the first professional paid soccer players. This skill ran in the family, as my cousin, Franck Leboeuf, the Chelsea player, became a world champion. Everyone in the family was interested in soccer but I never really got into it myself.

My parents didn't really know what to do with me when I tried to be an air force pilot but didn't make it. Like so many people, I was rejected because of my eyesight. But I was successful in getting into a hotel school in Strasbourg in Alsace, about two hours from home. And getting into that school was a success, because it was what's called a *concours* in French, which means it was only the best that got in. It was a boarding school. I was 15 at the time.

The first piece of advice I got was from the principal of the hotel school who told me on the first day that I wasn't wearing the right shoes, the right shirt, the right tie, that I didn't look good – and, most important, I didn't say "Hello" to him politely in the right way! He called me, "Sir, where are you going?". I said I was running to wherever I was running. He said, "Perhaps you have forgotten something". I looked blank, and he said, "Perhaps you have forgotten to say 'Good morning, sir?'". I'll never forget that one. Incidentally, you can catch me saying that to young people sometimes nowadays. Even some the best graduates from top hotel schools in Lausanne or Cornell, with maybe five years of studies behind them, cannot look you in the eye, smile and say "Good morning" or "Good afternoon". That is something that I was taught very early. And you know you have got only a few seconds to make a first impression.

It was a very strict school. Everything was scored out of 20. If you didn't have at least a 12 as your overall grade, you were thrown out; if you had any subject where your grade was below 5, you were thrown out. They were serious.

In English on my first trimester examination, I scored 4 out of 20 so I knew I would be out the door soon. 'Out the door' would be mean going back to the countryside, which I really didn't want. The English teacher said, "Philippe, it's up to you to make it happen". He told me to buy the book, *English in 90 Lessons*. Although it was a boarding school, some people would go home at weekends; I stayed in and I taught myself English, scholastic English. In the second trimester, I think I scored a 6 or 7 and, long story short, I finished the year at the top of the class. It taught me that, if you have strength and if you stick to it, you can make anything happen. Academically, it was difficult – but I made it. Essentially, my entire career revolved around 'you can learn'. Years later, I won the national prize for a self-taught person given by the Harvard Business School and *Les Grandes Écoles*, which is a little ironic, don't you think? At the time, the prize was given at the Senate – it was a big deal. So self-learning to me is very important.

At 17 and a half, I started working, at weekends, while still at hotel school. I worked in a restaurant as an apprentice waiter and I learned the hard way – the good way, like many people in the hotel business. One of my significant moments was in a *brasserie* in Alsace where I was working at the weekend. There were no computers at the time – just two sheets of paper for the two waiters, one of them was me, with an all cash system. I made a mistake and so, at the end of the day, after working 15 or 16 hours, I found owed money to the owner according to the accounts. So I decided that I would have to learn about finance. So my first lesson I learnt the hard way!

I was lucky after hotel school to get my start a big hotel, the Hôtel Concorde Lafayette in Paris, a 1,000-room hotel. I was working at night and went through the automation change to computers – that was extremely interesting, which people tend not to appreciate nowadays because it is so standard to have computers. I had a rough start there, although I had done well at school. It was my first job, and I was extremely young. One of the porters there was nice to me. He told me it was going to be tough, and he taught me – it's so obvious, but it needs to be said – to always tell the truth. That was the second piece of good career advice I received.

At the Hôtel Concorde Lafayette, I was totally inspired by the GM who had gone to Cornell; he did summer courses, but he had Cornell on his resumé. I said, "I want to go to Cornell too". So I went to the States, and became an immigrant, which is a good school too. I had to make a living so I gave French lessons, I became a French private tutor – and I got to take some courses at Cornell. Because of Cornell, I managed to work in another big hotel in New York, 700 bedrooms, the Parker Meridien. I was doing fairly well there, I had been there about three years, when a headhunter sent me a lovely letter – today perhaps it would be done by email – advertising a job at The Carlyle in New York. Because I was the person handing out the mail, I realised that the letter had been sent not just to me but also to all my assistants. I thought this guy was not too smart, but then I realised that if he was doing that multiplied by the 700 hotels in New York he was bound to get the people he wanted. Once I had gone through the process of interviews, one of the final interviews was at The Carlyle, which to me was like going from having a lovely Toyota to a Rolls Royce. At the time I was not self-confident enough to think that I might get the job but I got it and that's where my hotel education really took off.

My title was Executive Assistant Manager, which is a lovely title but means absolutely nothing – that was one of the first things I learnt! You can be a front of house supervisor with that title or actually be the GM or more. I thought I was number two – actually I was number three – it didn't dawn on me to check beforehand. But the number one and number two guys were top people and I learnt so much from them. I didn't have much contact with the number one guy, Dan Camp – he was more like the President or CFO. The number two at The Carlyle, Frank Bowling, became one of my first mentors. He had been at The Connaught in London as number two and then he was at The Ritz-Carlton in New York. Frank Bowling was the kind of guy who could call Betsy Bloomingdale or Nancy Reagan – I learnt so much from him and we became good friends. Frank managed The Carlyle during the day and I managed it during the evening shift.

For the owner, who held on to the old principles, this hotel was really his passion. His background was in the industry – at 15, his mother sent him to work in room service and the bar and he knew everything about his business by the time he was 17.

We had computers at the time – it was the USA in 1980 – but the owner came in one night and asked at reception, "Has Mr. X arrived?", and someone said "Who?". That's when he removed the computers. He said, "You guys need to understand about name recognition – goodbye computers!".

So we had to write everything by hand and, as soon as the guest was checked in, we would enter the information in the back office – for billing and so on. They only changed it back to computers less than 10 years ago – the hotel stayed without computers in the front of house all that time.

The Carlyle was, and still is today, one of the few hotels in the world that has staff in the elevator, the same as at Claridge's. Although the cabins are totally computerised, they kept a person in the elevator because that person knows your floor, can do chit-chat, can help on the floor, can help if you forgot your phone, you're running and he holds the elevator – those are the dimensions of service expected at that level.

So The Carlyle was a wonderful experience. I stayed there for three years. As executive in charge, I took care of the entertainment after dinner at the Café Carlyle. Woody Allen played regularly every Monday. We also had people like Bobby Short, Linda Carter and Eartha Kitt. I wish I had been there 20 years before! I was there in the late 1980s – the 1950s and 1960s must have been out of this world!

I was responsible for greeting the guests as they arrived and taking care of the dinner seating. It was all about first impressions: you have a few seconds to know who's who, to understand whether the guest is here on business or pleasure. The waiters had to understand too because we had heads of state on private visits, the rich and the famous, the poor and the important, or all of the above, coming to The Carlyle. It was very exciting.

My next move was from the big rooms / big ratio hotel to a smaller hotel, The Westbury, where I worked for an English company, Forte Hotels. I worked for Lord Forte, and then Rocco Forte, which opened my eyes to the importance of ROI and shareholder value. And there I was number two.

Then there was a rationalisation of costs and of people. We had five hotels in North America and put in a regional GM, which basically meant that I became a 'mini-GM'. And then France called me back to the Hôtel de Crillon.

At 36, I was GM of The Crillon in Paris, my first and long-awaited appointment as GM. I guess they knew they needed a French national because The Crillon at the time was the only hotel in Paris that would welcome heads of state. At The Carlyle, I must have greeted 50 or 100 heads of state. They also wanted a Frenchman with US experience, since the US was a huge market, and the owners at the time were the Taittingers, the champagne owners. And last, as you know, wine growers are very big sales people, so they wanted someone sales-friendly, in terms of their competence, and – *voilá* – I got the job. And I stayed there for seven years.

Then I was promoted, and went to corporate. But after four or five years of corporate work, I said, "I miss the clients, the relationships and you only get that as GM". So I got a fabulous job as a Regional GM with some corporate responsibility and responsibility for opening another hotel in Geneva. Through my career, I have become a little bit of an opening specialist.

While I was in this role, the entire business was sold and restructured and the President of the company and I lost our jobs. I told my best friend, who ran his own business. He just laughed and said, "You're crazy, calling to get sympathy. You need to understand what it is to be your own boss". I didn't understand – and then I got it after a year or a year and a half of searching for the right job.

Out of unhappiness, there's always something good for the future. I decided that I was interested in learning more about strategy and finance so I was able to do the equivalent of an MBA but, in France, it's more like two Master's degrees combined. I did a strategic Master's and a financial Master's at the age of 45. I did them in one year at the *École des Hautes Études Commerciales de Paris* (HEC), the only MBA programme at a top French university recognised in the US – and that was great. I also was working for some hotel people, who gave me projects so I was not bored! HEC demystified what it is to be a financier, because it is intimidating for people who are not specialists, and I put all my heart into strategy because that was my main interest. I think the initial hotel schooling we get is not enough; you have go back to school, like I did three times, for major schooling, so I bless the opportunity that I had.

I was lucky – but you also have to grab the luck when it is presented to you. I always grab. I am a bit of an opportunistic person, there's no shame to say it. There's also timing, you know – especially in the hotel business, which is tough and competitive.

❖

Claridge's is a beautiful institution, the epitome of the English hotel, so it was fun to be its French GM. Like the Hôtel de Crillon, or The Carlyle, where I worked also, it is one of those iconic well-known local hotels with its own challenge to install technology to meet the basic expectations of service today – but what a beautiful place! It's a classical environment in the middle of Mayfair, and I worked with a wonderful lady who used to be my client, Diane von Fustenberg, to create a deluxe suite with David Linley. The second thing I instigated was our

Christmas tree in the lobby with John Galliano, who was designing for Dior at the time. People now go to Claridge's just to see the Christmas tree. Because of the PR, it was a great success.

Claridge's always had exceptional levels of service, like every good hotel. We sent the Head Butler at Claridge's to Buckingham Palace; we did an exchange and learnt a lot from them – although I was not supposed to talk about it officially. Our big PR moment, of course, was the TV show. I was not for it but my boss at Maybourne wanted to do it. As GM, I would have preferred to preserve the confidentiality of my guests – but there is no doubt that it was great publicity and I think overall it has been very well received. Some clients were critical, because the mystique of "I can afford Claridge's", leads to "I want to be left alone. I don't want people to know everything" but on the other hand it's fun for the public to know. I think we'll see more and more of this kind of show.

These days I find myself being asked to make conference speeches by some of the world's best brands, but I think the bottom line is that you can't say that you have reached the top. You have to be willing always to learn, and to listen. Learning is also listening. You have got to listen to your clients more and more and more – much more than before. It's an essential part of our business.

But it's not enough now just to listen. A sommelier can't just name the Burgundy 1975 or whatever. Now he must sell it, he must explain it, he needs to know so much more because the person in front of him might be reading something on his smartphone or tablet where it says "1975 was not so good, but

1977 was good". So much information is out there so you have got to be aware and up-to-date. It's tough but that's what I think is exciting. I am very excited about my business.

Now I hire people more for their attitude than for their aptitude because I think technically being a hotelier is not like being a brain surgeon – it's more about people and interaction. I think you can teach a lot in that area but you cannot make a racehorse out of a mule. If someone is totally introverted, is too shy to say "Hello", it's going to be very hard to put him in the right place. This is a real issue because parents now push their kids into becoming a hotelier, perhaps because hotels have become very trendy, perhaps more in France than in the UK, but being a hotelier not easy since it's mainly about service.

I'm passionate about service – I even wrote a book about it, called *Service Incompris*! Nowadays, service is different from five or 10 years ago because we always have to change. For example, taxis in Paris don't understand service; they do not provide service; they will probably be killed by the Ubers of this world. Uber is interesting, because it provides a totally different service combined with amazing computer technology. It's actually mindboggling – paradigm-changing. The primacy of service is starting to be accepted a lot by the industry but I think we must keep service in our minds and ensure it remains strong.

Hotel school was my first experience of service. My mother pushed me. She was from the restaurant business, and I guess she knew I could go further as a hotelier. But I didn't understand service at first. I only started to get it in my first job where basically if you gave people good service, you got something back, some sort of happiness – sometimes you even got a tip! But even if you didn't get a tip, you got a smile. If I please you, somehow you are going to convey that pleasure back to me and that's really nice and I like to please people. I saw that right away in my first job: I could please simply by giving the right room assignment. I remember greeting TWA crew members: they were exhausted coming in off a long flight and simply to have their room ready, recognition of their name, recognition of what they needed – it was great.

And then we get to meet such wonderful people. That's the most exciting thing. Not only stars – because sometimes I am oblivious to stars – but very exciting people. That's what I like the most about my job.

Talking about people I have met, naturally I talk about the first one that really moved me: the Dalai Lama. I shook his hand when I greeted him at The Carlyle in New York. I felt that I got a brain scan – a total physical scan, everything at the same time, all in two seconds. His eyes were so brilliant and he was so genuine. There has to be something genuine inside a person like that. I got to meet the Dalai Lama twice – the second time was in India at a hotels conference and that was incredible too.

The second person that I was most moved by – I spent longer with him – was Michael Jackson. That was also at The Carlyle. He was almost not human, because he was so 'out there'. I don't know how to describe it; he was just very special. Another person who left a very strong impression on me was Bryan Ferry – so talented and elegant and full of energy. And when you meet these people, what's so exciting is that they are quite simple people.

Another thing you find in these kind of people – it's no secret – is that they are hard workers. Michael Jordan was Michael Jordan because he was the first one on the basketball court and the last one to leave training or practice. It's the same with Tiger Woods, the same thing. He was the best golfer I ever saw, but he trained. It is rare that top successful people are not also very, very hard workers.

My first big boss in New York, Stefan Simkovics – he works now for Four Seasons – impressed me because he taught me to be on the ground for the ease of running inspections and knowing what is happening. Today, for example, my real office is still in the lobby. My office is supposed to be on the fifth floor of The Mandarin Oriental but I chose to have a tiny cupboard in the lobby. It means I am available, no one has to wait five minutes for me to come downstairs, I see and hear everything that's going on. You know, people go on huge financial-based courses where they become capable of doing incredible cashflow projections, but they miss the nitty-gritty of our business, which is people, people and people. Being around the lobby is so important, it's where you get to meet the staff, where you get to know what's going on. You have to breathe your hotel and have your finger on its pulse. In an office on the fifth floor, you cannot know that.

Here at The Mandarin Oriental, I am promoting a luxury brand. It is hard to express but the hotel business is becoming like some top brands – going beyond hotels and restaurants and becoming a system of luxury that becomes a business. I think that's what our CEO, an incredibly smart man, is trying to do and I am so in sync with that vision.

Nowadays, with all the technology, people are searching for good human relations. For so many people, it goes beyond even the service aspect, it's about feelings and emotions – with no limits. And now, technology can help you give other dimensions to service that go beyond the hotel. To me, the hotel experience starts at home when the client is searching on the Internet, and somehow you have to leave a very good impression. As a result, he may change his habits and not stay at The Pierre any more and instead go to The Mandarin – that's the kind of thing we try to do. But without being cookie-cutter – because that to me is contrary to luxury hotels. For example, in Paris, at The Mandarin Oriental, we are still very Parisian. We have three architects – French architects – to uphold the material design of the exterior, because we are assiduous in keeping to the design of the hotel. For us, it is very important to encourage and have the Parisian crowd because the client staying with us expects to get a feel of France, not just a luxury hotel in a top city. And it's very hard to do!

What makes a great hotelier has changed a lot, I think. In today's market where they talk about hotels as assets, you have to be a bit of an entrepreneur for the financial part of it and in the creative part of it you have got to renew your business model quite often. But a great hotelier is someone who has a passion for this whole job. It's not something you do for money. It's a lifestyle. You have to not care about the hours, and you have to have passion for people generally – guests and staff alike.

In Paris, some luxury brands have come to us, asking me to teach them about people – for example, Hermès came and asked, "How did you open this hotel?". I couldn't believe it. But when you think about it, they are like us, they have got two seconds for a first impression. People are not as loyal as before, people are more fickle. Even in the hotel business, where Claridge's might have had three generations of a family staying, this is changing now. This is where our business model for the new Mandarin Oriental hotels is focused, not the traditional hotels like in Hong Kong, or in Bangkok, but the new hotels. We see that some people don't have allegiances – and there's the opportunity.

It is getting harder and harder to stand out from other luxury hotels – it's extremely difficult now. I still think service is the key, but even service evolves. For example, we were very good at me greeting and not missing any VIPs but now the very top VIPs prefer that you leave them alone, don't greet them, don't make a fuss about them – but the funny part is that they also want to be dead sure that you know who they are! And what they want or don't want. So it's very, very difficult!

It's a little like you going into a restaurant where you get the perception that even though they might not use your name, they know exactly who you are, they know you are coming for business, they know that you do not want to be interrupted every five minutes to meet certain service standards that are written in scripts somewhere. On the surface it doesn't look like VIP service – but it is a truly deep level of service, it's very refreshing when you receive it!

At a weekend for new staff recently, I explained that guests expect us to have the perfect decor, the perfect room, the perfect service, that what's on the plate is at the perfect temperature. But it's the other dimension, the emotional dimension, that we are very much about at The Mandarin Oriental. We focus on emotions linked to service, to somehow say, "I know you are here on strictly on business but by the time you leave tomorrow one of my colleagues will have been able to make you feel special". That's what people are looking for nowadays.

Great lobbies are what make a hotel world class! It's important to have a beautiful lobby, the right lighting, a certain I would say 'flow' – it's important to have the right flow. To take The Mandarin Oriental as an example, look at the way the floor is designed with two restaurants opposite each other and a big beautiful garden. Flows are important, there is surely an expertise behind them. Design is key – here in The Mandarin Oriental, we have the biggest rooms in Paris. In terms of bathroom design, bathrooms are now much bigger. Location is key – we see this in Paris. At The Mandarin Oriental, we are blessed with a wonderful location. London is a little bit easier because there seems to be more than one 'centre', either you are in Knightsbridge or Mayfair or you are one of the new hotels that have opened around Canary Wharf. Nowadays, unfortunately, it is important to be part of some sort of international brand. If you are a standalone hotel, like Gleneagles, you can be part of Leading Hotels of the World, which helps to balance the huge infrastructure of the big hotel groups.

My advice to someone starting out who wants to go all the way to the top? Work – work and work and work. Never get discouraged; and I know it's very clichéd, but failures are good for learning – if you learn from them!

Marketing can start on an iPhone, at home, maybe a month before the customer travels. And it finishes again at home, perhaps again on the customer's iPhone because he receives a survey. So what does this mean for a young person in the industry in terms of them being a marketer? Hotels in the luxury world are becoming more than just hotels, so if you think marketing is taking a great picture of a beautiful bedroom with flowers and champagne, like we have all done, it's not that! Today, great ads allow you to convey the message of intuitive service – efficient and discreet service, this is key. And then to go beyond that, brands in general and luxury brands are moving to this next step. I was talking to one of the top salesmen of a major luxury car brand. When you talk to him, he doesn't talk about the car. You almost have to beg him to talk to you about the car. He talks about the beauty of this and the craftsmanship of that. You really have to insist that he talks about the car – and that's deliberate. He wants to create a feeling of trust, something between you and him, because it's no longer just the salesperson and the car. Take the name TrustHouseForte, which many young people don't even know of nowadays. There was a key message in the name – a House you could Trust brought to you by Forte. The word 'trust' is gone in many places today, replaced by other dynamics: price, cost, brand, etc.

To a young person, I would say also, "Travel". You must travel. Do not stay in England, or France, or Switzerland. Even if you are English, go to Asia; when you come back to England, you will have grown, you will have learnt a lot.

We need to talk about the environment too. You cannot just be in the hotel business. The Mandarin Oriental is a young hotel but in France it has achieved the 'high quality environmental' (*haute qualité environnementale*) accolade – the only Palace to do so. You cannot go into the hotel business and ignore the environment, you have got to embrace it for many reasons – your employees and increasingly your clients, they want to know there is an environmental campaign behind the hotel.

What is great service? Great service has no limits. Always as a joke – but it's not really a joke – I say, "The only limits to service are legality and the comfort of the other guests!". At Claridge's, we always used the word 'timeless' to describe service. But time is an issue now for many people. People are a little stressed about time, and even in a luxury environment you have to have some awareness of time to help your guests de-stress. For example, in a resort hotel like I am opening in Marrakesh now, we know people are going to arrive from London or Paris a bit stressed out and, if we do a good job, then two, three or four days later they won't have that stress. But you must somehow anticipate and know that and act on it.

Claridge's used to be a typical leisure destination; now people are staying there for work, or for both leisure and work and you have to balance that. Here, 75% of my guests are in Paris for leisure.

Hoteliers have to change because of the need for service number one. I always talk about service. Hoteliers also need to embrace technology, totally, without letting technology take over like in some hotels where it is hard to close the curtains because you cannot find the right switch! Hoteliers need to be inventive. For example, I use retail as a source of inspiration. In the Burberry flagship shop in London, you can buy a dress or a coat without talking to anyone if you want to; you simply use a terminal. Should you be able to do that for a suite, as a guest? I don't know, but I don't think you can dismiss it as bad or say that the hotel experience is only about the human rapport. It's a changing world; our children now have a little screen that they use for everything. We have to change!

My most memorable day happened at The Crillon. I am also an athlete, you have got to know that about me, I am crazy about biking. So I knew Lance Armstrong pretty well, he used to come to The Crillon where I was working at that time. Each time he would invite an incredible crowd and he would talk about charity and do a lot of work for LiveStrong, which is a charity against cancer. I do something similar for children who have cancer, it is called *A Chachun son Everest*, To Each His Own Everest. One of the people invited was Robin Williams, who had always been a guest of the Hôtel D'Orsay. I was nervous about greeting him, especially because I recognised that he was coming here because he had been invited and not necessarily by his own choice. Anyway, to welcome him, I decided to fly the Texan flag, the one star flag for the Lone Star state, on top of the hotel. This was actually illegal because The Crillon is one of the few hotels in Paris that received heads of state and it is only when you are receiving a head of state that you are allowed to fly a flag other than the French flag, but sometimes you have to take some risks! Robin Williams arrived. He looked at the flag, he looked at me up and down a bit, then he looked up at the flag again and said, "I have never stayed in a one star hotel before"! And that was in front of 30 journalists and photographers, and I said to myself "Wow! That's why that guy is who is he is!". And whether it was him or Woody Allen who used to imitate me in at the Café Carlyle in New York, all these people who are so famous are just so natural, it's amazing.

But for students in this business, remember that these people are their own person. Do not cross the line. Remember that they are clients. You are privileged to meet and serve them. You are still the employee. Service has to be the reality wherever you are. You are still at the service of the guest. You must never forget that the client always remains the client and you are there to serve the client. Those would be my closing words!

NATHALIE SEILER-HAYEZ

The Connaught Hotel, London

Hôtel Lutetia, Paris
Rosewood Hotels & Resorts
Radisson Champs Elysées, Paris
Hôtel du Louvre, Paris
The Regent Grand Hotel, Bordeaux
The Connaught Hotel, London
Beau Rivage Palace Hotel, Lausanne

You cannot be inspired, if you stay only
in your own hotel behind closed doors.

I was born in Geneva, Switzerland. I didn't have any brothers or sisters; I was an only child.

In the 1950s, my father, who is now 95 years old and still keeping in great shape, created the *Hotel and Travel Index*, this big book that every year became larger and larger, where all of the hotels of the world advertised. At the time, it was extraordinary. So I could say I was born into the world of hotels.

My parents travelled a lot on business, and sometimes I had the chance to go with them. So I think very early I was used to hotels and being surrounded by international people everywhere. If I had to summarise how I grew up, it was in an international surrounding. It was not that we lived in different countries but we did travel a lot.

When my parents travelled, I went to a special school in the Swiss mountains, which gave me an amazing community. There were lots of other kids there, so with no brother or sister, it was amazing for me. I have only fabulous memories of it. The fact that I love the mountains and nature probably comes from that time. Nowadays, every time I need to re-energise, I go back to the mountains.

I think I had a wonderful childhood. Probably not an ordinary childhood but wonderful. When my parents were there, I got a lot from them, a lot of love. At school I had a good balance, nothing special in terms of study.

But very early, my career became clear in my head. I was fascinated with hotels, by the guest aspects in particular. I remember a trip with my parents to Thailand, when I was 17. They brought me to the Āman resort, which had just opened. This was where I realised I was going to become a hotelier because I wanted to run a hotel like that one day. To put it in perspective, at 17 years old, you are very impressionable … the blue sky, the blue sea, the extraordinary bouquet, everything is extraordinary. I think it was the sense of how everything at the resort made me feel! It was just not about the beauty of the design, which was wonderful, but at Āman you felt connected emotionally. The staff connected with me and I think this is really basic. The sense of welcome and all of the little touches that were so special for me, for a 17 year old girl – it goes back to what it is all about: empathy. It's about how the staff make you feel more than anything.

Growing up in Switzerland is special, even more so probably 30 years ago. At that time, Switzerland was really this kind of heaven, a super-special environment. You need never lock the door of your house or your car; you would never have a robbery; it was very secure. And it was not that I was specially privileged, it was more about feeling safe – and I think you only realise that when you leave.

And the Swiss do have a reputation for hospitality; it's part of what the country used to be very good at. Perhaps I am being a little too hard when I say 'used to be'. I think we used to have amazing places run from generation to generation but, of course, like everywhere, it is becoming globalised and we are losing this type of service. And yet you still have family-run hospitality businesses. They are still part of what the country is known for, as well as the chocolate and watches! We still have amazing hotels in Switzerland.

So when the time came to figure out what to do for a programme of study, I didn't have to think too long: it had to be the Lausanne Hotel School. Obviously, my travel experiences with my parents were a big influence but I can tell you that, the moment I arrived at the school, I knew it was for me. If I could go back and do it again, I'd start tomorrow!

In the hotel school, there was again that international thing of people coming from all over the world. I really don't like being among only people of my own background. I enjoy international people, so I think my enjoyment of Lausanne came partly from that. Also the discipline at the time in Lausanne was fabulous – they expected a man to wear a suit and a tie and ladies to wear appropriate outfits – and we were 18 or 19 year old students in school!

And then I enjoyed the combination of something very practical combined with theory – for hospitality, it is critical to have practical and theory side-by-side. You have to be very attentive so that you both understand and can do. I enjoyed that balance. You have a lot of practical work. At the beginning, working in the kitchen can be really hard. Suddenly you arrive in the kitchen, which you have never seen before, you don't know how a kitchen works – but you are here to work. You must do things that you have never done before. You are here to study – and you may be good at that – but you also need to understand how all the processes work. You may not learn how to cook – unfortunately, although we spent a lot of time in the kitchen, I am not good at it – but thanks to the training, I understand how a cook or a chef thinks. And that's what you really need to understand.

I think that the whole four years at hotel school gave me a very good foundation. The problem, though, is that when you leave this type of school, supposedly the best in the world, you suddenly go back to reality and it's not going to be as GM. And this is where, for some people, sometimes the challenge can be. This is the problem with these big schools: they always make you think that you are at the top and that you are going to run the world, which maybe one day you will, if you are good – but not just because you went to this school!

But at Lausanne, we also learnt how to have fun, how to enjoy life. It's not a small thing; you need to learn about life. You need to learn what hotel life is about. You party but then the next day you must be ready in your black tie, be properly dressed, with everything organised. For me, this discipline, this international world, this combination between theory and practical, I found it all wonderful.

And then, of course, we had the placement – six months at that time, it has changed now – where you had to go into a training position in a hotel, a real hotel. My first placement was in the kitchen, six months just in the kitchen! But now I don't regret doing it because again to really understand the mentality of the cook, of the chef, how you need to talk to him, how he thinks, the problems he has to handle, you need to do this. It was a tough six months but I want to say nothing negative. I did my placement in a lovely hotel in Lausanne. I had a great time, the owner was very nice to me and I got out of this placement what I wanted – which was to really understand the chef.

My real interest was the guests, because that's what I see as the most important part of a hotel. You need to have this passion; it's not like running a normal business. We run an emotional business. I love guests but also my staff. I love people and I love developing people. There is a real satisfaction when people who have been working with you come and tell you as Paul Heery, my Operations Manager here at The Connaught, did not long ago, "I am going to Gleneagles as their new GM". As much as I hated to lose him, there is nothing better than seeing people grow. This is part of our mission. The role of the general manager must focus on the staff. Sure, the general manager must focus on the guests, particularly on the guests, and of course they also must have a love for food and wine. But, above everything, the general manager's job is about people. If you do not have this passion for people, then I think it's going to be very difficult to be a top class general manager. Yes, there are GMs who can run a hotel perfectly well without being that people-oriented, but the hotel is always run to a good standard not to a luxury standard.

Lots of people have inspired me in my career but I think it was in Lausanne that I learnt to work hard, to make things happen, to succeed. If you want to get a diploma, I think you need to be well-organised, to be able to organise a project, and be able to balance everything.

Sometimes I feel that an academic approach can help me a lot in getting the structure right. So I have done management courses in my career, as well as other kinds of business courses. This is important because the way we run hotels now is very different to 20 years ago. If you look at the general manager's role in particular, it has evolved big time – because it had to! In the old days, it was like the military: the general manager had all of the soldiers around him and they expected him to tell them what to do. This is how I was trained: the GM was the head and the rest were soldiers – and when I arrived here at The Connaught five years ago, this is what I found! For me, it is impossible to run a business like that. It's not a one-man-show; it is not possible for one person to know everything. The people around me know the business better than I do; they know their area much better than I could ever do. So competent staff are vital for real hospitality and a much flatter structure, not a hierarchy, is the best way to manage today. Managing people is critical. If there is a crisis, it needs a decision right now! This is what management is about. You need to be able to decide quickly – and bring people with you. Here the decisions must be made in a much more participative way so I think that having a little more academic background helps in my career to ensure the structure always works to the benefit of the hotel.

The last placement that I did was in Hong Kong. It was very inspiring and it really gave me a sense of Asia, especially the quality of service. I recalled my Āman experience, the Thai and the way they are eager to serve and to please. So, for six months, I was Assistant Food & Beverage Director at The Conrad in Hong Kong. The placement gave me a very good understanding of the department and also a sense of quality, the extra things that created perfection.

When I graduated from Lausanne, I started my career in Sales & Marketing in Paris, as a sales representative for Concorde Hotels for Switzerland and Germany – being Swiss, I speak German. So they gave me this sales and marketing title and I thought, "What am I doing here?". There is nothing in a book, no blueprint, no course of study at Lausanne that prepared me for this work!

But I must have been doing something right because they promoted me to be in charge of the London market. I had good people around me in Sales & Marketing at the regional office who guided me. At this stage, I think I only got about 30% of what it was I was supposed to do. Then they gave me North America, so I went back and forth a lot to the US starting now to understand the role more, dealing with agencies, tour operators, HR and so forth. That was when I started building a lot of great relationships with top travel agents who have followed me in my career and helped me to progress.

For me, learning the sales role was very important in my professional development. But I knew also that, by taking the sales route, I would have to miss out other parts of the hotel business, some of them parts of the business that I really enjoyed. What this taught me is that no general manager can ever have or learn it all.

Within five years, I was Sales & Marketing Director. Because I was in the US so often, I thought, "I want to work in the US and understand their way of doing things, to understand what exactly is this 'American efficiency'". And so I left Paris and joined Rosewood Hotels, still in Sales & Marketing. I was based in New York in charge of the Caribbean region. Then I came to understand it was less about whether to sell Paris or the Caribbean; in the end it is about understanding how to sell and the relationships, as well as the networking. I loved every minute of it.

When I joined Rosewood, it was a very small group, just starting to develop the brand, but it was also an amazing hotel collection. This is where I really learnt all about 'luxury' and what it means. Today, when I'm running The Connaught, I ask myself about our guests: "Who are they? What do they want?". The service we provide must be based on that – and only that. You know sometimes people come to me and say, "We need to change the china" and I ask, "Do we really need to change the china or is it because you just want to please yourself? What do the guests want?". 'Let's change the china because I'm bored with it' is not a reason to change the china. Decisions must be from the guest's point of view always.

I think this is where I really started soul-searching and thinking to myself, "Because you understand marketing, you understand this so much better. You understand what guests want, because you travel all the time. You see a lot of agents, you see a lot of guests of course, and you are interacting with them all the time. You see a lot of different hotels which is where you get your own inspiration". Travelling and visiting new places and new properties excites me. For example, I am flying this weekend for business, to go to a roadshow in the US, and we are planning to visit and stay in a new property in New York – and I cannot wait! The property opened two months ago. I really want to see their service level, to see their marketing, to see how they are they using technology – just to see what's new. You cannot get inspired, if you stay only in your own hotel behind closed doors.

It is really important because we try to adapt everything to the nationality of the guest we are welcoming. For example, in the Far East, the fruit bowl is not just a bowl with fruit; it is a work of art, and it is the centre of the table, the centre of attention. For them, the fruit bowl has to be amazing.

If you really want to be bespoke, you can't do that without having a strategy and that strategy needs to be in-house. This is the only way that you can deliver the right service because every nationality and every culture is different. We must connect with that.

Everyone is so different and sometimes hotels don't do things simply because of the lack of knowledge of what people do or don't want. I was visiting a hotel in Paris a little while ago, which had mirrors all over and I was thinking, "OK, looks nice but, in five years, when China is supposed to be your biggest market, how will your mirrors work with feng shui?". This is so important and we must learn that, understand that and make sure we do it right for the guests. We must constantly be asking, "So how do you do that?". This is our

biggest challenge now: to be strategic and not to be reactive because today we all need to be so quick and not just driven by the day-to-day operation of the hotel. You simply have to have a clear vision and that means knowing what the hotel will look like in five years' time. Again, that is why you must travel, see new hotels and develop a plan that is informed by trends and not just what we like ourselves.

I was in the USA on 9/11. I was working in New York at that time, and the office I was in looked directly out on the Twin Towers. I saw everything from the window. I saw the first tower collapsing and I have to say it was an absolute trauma. I think it changed something within me.

It was a beautiful morning, everything as normal. I left my apartment in the same way as I usually did. I stopped at the bagel shop on the corner and grabbed my coffee. I arrived in my office. I remember I was on the phone to my father and I said, "Oh my God! One tower is on fire! There's a big fire. There's chaos". He said, "Oh, maybe we will see that later back in Switzerland on the television" and then I interrupted, "I see a plane!". I said to my father, "My God, that's an American plane". I could see the second plane and I thought it was the Fire Department coming with water to stop the fire. Then I saw it crash. I thought it was a crash, an accident. Please don't misunderstand me – but if it is an accident, it is somehow 'acceptable', it is an accident. Accidents happen. Maybe 15 minutes later, we found out that it was a terrorist attack. So, of course, the whole thing becomes very different.

The image that stays in front of me every time I think of it was the twin buildings collapsing. The Twin Towers, the tallest in New York, right in front of you. One minute, they are there, the next they are falling, gone! And then it's really you, you are there, you are a witness.

We had to leave the building. We came out into the street into the chaos and suddenly I looked at myself and I realised I was running like everyone else with my shoes on my head, protecting myself. You suddenly realise how small you are – your life can go now, it might be over – and that's very frightening and defining. You become conscious that we are on an island in New York. Everyone wanted to go next to the water, to leave. We were all running to get away as quickly as we can.

I stayed with the team in Manhattan. Nobody wanted to be alone. Suddenly, you are aware of the lack of noise, the silence. I don't think I would be lying if I was to tell you I walked from the office to my house and, in that 30 minutes or so, there was not one car, or one single noise. You could hear the wind but it was dead. It was just awful, awful. And then the smell, the smell was dreadful. It took forever for that to go.

And after this whole thing, you suddenly realise, "I have to travel, be amongst people, and to go home I have to go through security at the airport". The fear, how to manage the fear! Suddenly, you just want to go back home, where you belong, with your loved ones and this really made me feel that this was now my time to come back home. So my move back to Europe was much more driven by personal reasons than professional ones. I witnessed this very dark side of our world.

I came back to Paris again and I was still in love with Sales & Marketing. I had two possibilities: to go into Corporate Sales &

Marketing or into a property. I am a people person. I like strategy but not as much as I like people. I was super-lucky because the GM of a lovely hotel knew me and was looking for a number two. I wasn't qualified to be a number two because my operational background was only really what I had learnt back in Lausanne. But he said to me, "This is not about having an operational background. I think you can get there. I think you have the right human skills. I believe in you. You will be in charge of the strategy for Sales & Marketing – and you will be my number two". That was extraordinary – without him, they wouldn't have given me the chance. That was in the Hôtel du Louvre, a lovely hotel, just the right size. It is also special for me because it was where I met my husband!

My husband was Head Concierge at the Hôtel du Louvre. We started going out together only at the end of my four years at the hotel. It would have been impossible to have a relationship while we both worked there.

My time as number two at the Hôtel du Louvre was extraordinary for me because I learnt so much about operations. But then I could really see good negotiation and good leadership skills coming into play that I realised I had naturally. And probably also, coming from a Sales & Marketing background, I knew how to sell so I knew how to sell change to my people and this is really where I started to say, "Ahh, I am so glad I made this decision". On the operations side, I didn't find it that hard. The reason why was because I had seen so much in so many different hotels so there was a lot of stuff I could bring to the table by taking the guest's view – for example, in a bedroom, I would always sit on the bed like a guest. I always come back to the guest, the guest.

Emotional intelligence is important; it summarises it all. I think emotional intelligence is as much as maybe 80% of success when you are lucky enough to work with an amazing product like I have here at The Connaught. The emotional intelligence is not coming from you, it's coming from your staff. My job is about creating the culture and the biggest challenge or question here is "How do I make sure this culture travels down?". It's a constant behaviour thing. It's not about skills – you must have productivity, of course – but a great attitude is fundamental. How do you bring a glass to a guest? What's your attitude and your behaviour towards the guest when you bring that glass? Sustaining this delivery is the key thing. It's the consistency. It's partly art and partly science – the science is how to do it, but the art is in the delivery and especially in the consistency of the delivery.

I spend most of my time working with people on the whole people thing. If you are true, you have to empower people; if you are too hierarchical, it won't allow them to be empowered. Yes, you must have your processes but I believe the people in charge in each area must act like it's their own because the staff are going to be the ones to deliver the service. I am always shocked by the amount of time we spend with department heads in meetings and not with the doorman, because the doorman knows so much more about the guests! Instead of spending time with the doorman, you are going to be with the financial controller – why? The purpose of the back office is to grab all of the information that the line staff have about our guests. This is absolutely key, because often they know more than we do. We decide we want to build a new programme, a new something, without even asking them – why?

❖

I came back to Paris, spent four years as number two, learning about operations, understanding guests better – and then I was approached by Radisson, who asked me to be the GM of a really, really lovely property in Paris, The Radisson Champs Elysées, a boutique hotel but a real jewel! But it was a strange fit with their brand, which at that time was represented by Rezidor on the ground. It was a boutique hotel, very small, only 65 rooms, no banqueting or anything. It was a shame that the brand did not fit the property because it was an amazing experience. I think they came to me because of my sales and marketing background and I think they also wanted to have my personality to put an individual stamp on it just like you welcome someone into your home. They used me and I say 'used' in quotes but, for me, on the operations side, it was the best thing I have ever done because this is where I learnt how to really manage a hotel. In a small boutique hotel, as GM you see everything. So I quickly learnt exactly which costs were coming from who and how. I learnt about maintenance, which is not my forte, not where naturally I go. I had to because it is not like I had a big executive committee with a number one, number two, number three – it was me and the few heads of department. So I really had to play very hands on – and I learnt so much about all of the things that I needed to learn. On the other hand, of course, I was able to work with the guests, with the clients, which was an amazing experience.

I got pregnant and I had my first child, so that was kind of complicated. I stopped work just three weeks before because, as GM, "that's the problem with a woman sometimes". And a month after, I was back! So it was not like my owner could say anything. I was married to the right man, who helped me so much. I always say I wouldn't be here without his support. It would have been impossible.

Then after that, still through Rezidor, since this Radisson was really the jewel of the company, even as small as it was, and with my Rosewood luxury background, they proposed that I open The Regent in Bordeaux, now The Grand Hotel. Of course, for my next job, I was dreaming I would get a place like The Plaza Athenée in Paris or The Connaught in London, but I knew it would be too much of a step. I knew would need to go as number two into one of those hotels or as GM in a second city. So I took the opportunity in The Regent.

I managed the opening and then the hotel for three years. That was just a lot of experiences: the history, the culture, putting the people in the right places, what an opening is all about and then to position the property as a leading hotel of the world. In Bordeaux, the property was really amazing, a real palace but not in the right location. I spent most of my time promoting the destination, working to get the average rate that I was supposed to get. It's not easy when you are used to selling Paris or London or New York! So there was a big sales and marketing role in order to position the hotel as a destination.

And, while I was in Bordeaux, our second child was born – again, I took only a very short break before returning to work. But, in the end, Bordeaux is not a big city, and so after three years, I decided I wanted to go back to the big city: to Paris.

I got a big city, but instead of Paris, it was London – and that was even better. It was big jump to a fabulous hotel here at The Connaught. I think again it is about being at the right place at the right time. And also it's about having an owner who knows exactly what the property needs. They wanted it to have a personality, and I think my profile fitted well with the 120 rooms at The Connaught. It was actually my friend, Philippe Leboeuf, who used to run Claridge's at that time, who now runs The Mandarin Oriental in Paris – he's in the book! – who brought me to the company, because he used to be my CEO when I worked in Paris. Philippe and I have worked in several hotels together.

I arrived at The Connaught, to find that that the main hotel was run separately from the spa, which was run by Āman. There were four or five companies within the one hotel – so complicated. It took nearly a year to start figuring all that out and to put people together, to put the right people together, to unite them around one single objective. The most challenging thing for me was that a boat can only have one captain. That's nothing to do with ego at all; it's simply human nature. If you have two heads or three heads, people take advantage of that and then the place becomes unmanageable. And this is what I found when I arrived. It was not manageable.

It took me the first year to understand what I had and where I wanted to get it to; it took me a second year to bring the team and the structure to where I wanted them. We brainstormed together to decide the ideal structure and then looked to find the right people – structure first, people second. It was almost starting from scratch, although we had some very good people already in place. In a way it was good, because we didn't have to make many compromises. And we had the opportunity to revisit the structure and to make it much more flat than it used to be. Then I brought everything into one big division, one big team. Next, we built what we call a 'customer value proposal', which is all based on who is our guest, what do they want, what kind of service are we going to deliver? Now our aim is to offer the 'art of living well', which we translate through a sense of place, heritage, modernity and a very high level of service. Each area has a specific customer value proposal with an action plan. Within this frame, the manager is totally empowered to do things the way they want. I think the more empowered your people are, the more they can deliver. I think I said this earlier but the people who make the extraordinary happen are usually the people who are close to the guests, but they are usually less well paid and they are the people with whom you are not interacting with enough. The challenge as General Manager is how to make sure that these people have all of the right tools to create this extraordinary experience? So I spent a lot of time on people and I continue to do so. This is the biggest part of my job: people.

What makes The Connaught so special I think is the combination of its location and its people – their common vision, their empowerment and their motivation to deliver the right service. We always go back to people. Yes, we have an amazing product: it's a mix of heritage, modernity and art. It's fascinating – but without the human touch, what is there actually at The Connaught? We want guests to feel comfortable, welcomed, everything needs to be easy and seamless for them – we work very, very hard on all of these criteria. And our training comes from the management of the property. That makes a big difference for the new starter arriving at The Connaught; their first day of induction is delivered by two members of management – one of them a member of the executive committee and the other the person in charge of the area in which the starter will be working. That's a powerful message!

I learnt a lot during my career. Every single day almost, there is something that you learn. First, I think that, without your team, you are nothing. Second, you need to stay humble; you are not a guest, you are not an owner, you are here to serve people in the same way as any member of staff. Third, forget "I have the right …"; you do not have the right, you are here to serve people.

To get to the top, the first thing is that you need to work hard, there is no secret. If you just want a short cut, there isn't one! Yes, a little luck of course is important. If you work hard and you are a positive person, the positive brings you more positives and your star is going to be even stronger. I have always believed in myself in my professional life – I have always had this little thing inside me telling me, "That's good". This confidence – and confidence doesn't mean arrogance – drives you to do the right thing and that's important. People are so quick to tell you how bad you are, to tell what you have done wrong. If you tell me 10 times, "How beautiful you are!", in 10 seconds I will have forgotten that; but if you tell me just once, "My God, you are so ugly!", I will remember that for the rest of my life. If you focus too much on the negative, you can lose yourself and you cannot go on and then you cannot go to the top, I think. So you need to have a certain amount of self-confidence in what you are doing, trusting your gut-feeling to continue going, to keep the negative away. Also integrity is important: everything I have always done has always been for the people and for the business.

What makes a hotel world-class is the same thing that makes the difference between a good designer and a genius. It's easy to make a room, a bar or a lobby look nice – but to make it fabulous requires a genius. Even when it's fabulous, there still a huge gap between that and perfection. And then, how do you go from perfect to above perfect?

To do that you have to surround yourself with people who are perfect in their area, who are much better than you and not to be afraid that they are going to take over. I know that, yes, one day, someone will take over my job – good for him or for her – but in the meantime, if I have developed that person to the point where they can take over, I will have done something good.

Technology is definitely an element of the future of luxury hotels – but it's about finding the right balance between the technology and the human elements. The human side is so important. I see this because so many businesses come and steal our staff. More and more, these big businesses, these big brands, are looking at the service levels in hospitality and seeking to replicate them. Retail can learn so much from hospitality – and they do! Now you don't go to buy a Cartier watch, you go for an experience, you have someone like in hospitality who opens the door …

My advice to someone already in the business aiming for the top is to travel as much as you can, get inspired by luxury brands, don't stay only in your own area. For me, getting inspired is really the thing. Right now we are all focusing on these millennium people. Who are they? How do they think? What's the future? They don't want a desk in their bedroom, they want to be downstairs being part of a community – so how does that translate to my own hotel? I think you can understand this only by being a step ahead and, for that, you need to go out, outside your own hotel, to be inspired. So on the one hand, you need to have the right people in the right places in the hotel to make sure that you have the right processes and services delivered in the right way. On the other hand, you need to go out, to look outside, to think outside the box, because otherwise very quickly you can be out of the game. Don't be afraid of being creative, of being inspired by a different brand. Look at how Burberry is developing, borrowing from lots of different areas. And most important, as a leader at the top you need a vision, a clear vision … and of course, work hard – and stay true to yourself.

My stand-out day was at the beginning of my career. I was Sales Director in Paris at the Hôtel Lutetia. It was my first weekend as duty manager; I was 24, not long out of hotel school. It was 1998 and the Paris riots were happening. At 2 o'clock in the morning, they called me, "Nathalie, rioters are arriving into The Lutetia. What do we do?". The rioters had destroyed La Coupole – Le Brasserie de la Coupole – with fire. There were no police around. It was chaos. The rioters came into the hotel, we couldn't stop them. There were not that many, I would say no more than 50, so it was a manageable group. I came down and there were all of these people in the extraordinary lobby of The Lutetia. I stood up on a chair and I invited them all around and I said, "I represent the management of the hotel. But I am also Nathalie, a person. I cannot do a lot for you. What I can do for you now is to make sure you have some food, that you have some drinks". I was lucky, they all listened. We spent the night from 2 o'clock until 5.30 in the morning together. We served them breakfast at 5 o'clock and that was the deal: "We'll give you breakfast but then the hotel is going to open and you are going to go" and they all went! They thanked me for the breakfast. The staff were really good. We asked the pastry chef to come in to serve at 5 o'clock. And we served the rioters in the same way as we always do, what we would have done with a guest – you should have seen that! Then very quickly the TV people came, and the radio people. I didn't know at the time that I had to refer communications to PR; I just did it. And it went down very well – so it ended up being a very good communication thing. But I just acted from instinct – from gut-feeling and instinct and empathy. It was an extraordinary night.

But being a General Manager is extraordinary. Sometimes, I wish everyone had my job! You work hard but you have such a wonderful life. I think you get a chance to live a very full life: sometimes you are an architect, sometimes you are a cook, sometimes you are a marketing person and sometimes you are just the person looking after the toilets! Lots of things happen that are just predictable and then the extraordinary happens! So, if you do not want to have a routine job … I think if people knew what we do on a day-to-day basis, they would queue up to be a General Manager – it's really true!

MICHAEL DAVERN

The K Club, Kildare

TrustHouseForte

The K Club, Kildare

Fancourt Estate & Country Club, South Africa

Sandy Lane, Barbados

My job is to interfere!

I was born in 1967 and grew up in Cashel, County Tipperary, where there was one of the finest tourist attractions in Ireland: the Rock of Cashel. So at a very young age, I was meeting tourists on the streets and was first exposed to tourism. There was a powerful culture in the community about being tidy, because we were a showcase for visitors, and there was a pride in tourism and hospitality.

In the town – seven or eight doors down and across the road – was The Cashel Palace Hotel, an extraordinary hotel in its heyday. Owned by a group of investors including Vincent O'Brien, it shared that culture of great achievement in horseracing. Celebrities came to stay there: I can remember as a child that Larry Hagman, 'JR' from *Dallas*, stayed in The Cashel Palace. The hotel would later be owned by Ray Carroll, who opened The K Club in 1991 and would become a mentor of mine.

Joan Davern had a pub in the centre of the town. In the 1970s and early 1980s, when there were no gastropubs, no pub food, nothing like that, hers was the sort of pub where you got sausage rolls freshly baked, apple pie and cream, coffee from a pour-over machine with fresh whipped cream, not milk, and the best 'toasted special' in Ireland – they claimed the toasted special was invented there! My aunt ran the pub, because her husband, Don Davern, had died quite young. He had been a politician and in the Cabinet, in Dublin. In those days, when the Taoiseach (Irish Prime Minister) Jack Lynch was heading down to Cork at weekends, he would hold 'kitchen Cabinet' meetings in Davern's bar – so there would have been real entertainment and hospitality going on then!

My aunt Recie also had a pub and lounge bar in Thurles, which we visited, of course. And as a family, we used to visit another aunt of mine, Joan, who is married to Tony Breen, who

owned The Ard Rí Hotel in Waterford. We used to visit there
for Sunday lunch. At the time, my cousins lived in the hotel –
to me, it was like the Arthur Hailey novel, *Hotel*!

I also have great memories from childhood of The Cliff
House Hotel in Ardmore. My grandmother, Mary Davern – a
formidable businesswoman – would go there for a couple of
months in summer and my father and mother would take us
there to visit on a Saturday or Sunday. Sometimes, we would
stay for a few days. At the time, the hotel was owned by Frank
Nugent and run by Lilia Grant, who was the Manager. The
dining room had a wooden floor and oval-shaped windows
that looked out on the magnificent bay. We used to love the
gardens by the cliff; my grandmother would spend hours in
those beautiful gardens and that was where you would
inevitably find her when you arrived. It's a great hotel now,
having been transformed by Barry O'Callaghan, with a
Michelin star restaurant under the management of Adriaan
Bartels. Coincidently, my sister-in-law Siobhan was the
Deputy Manager there with Adrian when it reopened in its
current form.

Mary Davern also introduced us to restaurants. For special
occasions, we would be brought to Chez Hans in Cashel,
founded by Hans Matthiae in a converted Gothic church at the
foot of the Rock of Cashel. People travelled from all over
Munster and further to dine there and while, in its second
generation now, it continues to enjoy an excellent reputation, it
was something extremely special 35 to 40 years ago. I'm sure
that Cashel, Chez Hans and The Cashel Palace influenced
many people to join the hotel and hospitality business – one of
those was the Michelin star chef, Kevin Thornton, who like me
grew up only a few doors from both Chez Hans and The
Cashel Palace.

Both my parents were teachers: my father was the vice principal at the Christian Brothers' school in Cashel and my mother taught in the vocational school in Killenaule. My mother was very involved in the community in many ways, much more so than we ever realised until she passed away in November last. My father was very modest, quite shy, I think, and yet highly respected in the community. As a teacher, he liked people who showed potential but for some reason weren't able to excel. He took people like that under his wing and tried to work with them in school. He was tremendously interested in the rest of the world, in politics around the world, whether it was Africa or the Middle East, conflict, wars, what caused them. He was almost like a walking encyclopaedia. Before Google, he would have been Google! He literally visited the world from his house every day and was as knowledgeable about places as if he had visited them the day before – just through reading! He could tell you about the entire world but never went there, which I think was what encouraged me to travel. And when the Office of Public Works took over the Rock of Cashel to open it up to the public, he became a guide because he was so interested in history and he knew so much about it. I guess, without realising it, he was in the tourism business himself!

School for me was the Christian Brothers' school in Cashel, primary school and secondary school. I never went away from home until after my Leaving Cert. I think it was a combination of the experience of visiting the hotel in Waterford, seeing tourism at home in Cashel, and then being exposed to my cousins, two of whom went to the Shannon College of Hotel Management and went to Switzerland on placement, which sounded very glamorous, that led me to think, "I want to work in a hotel. I want to travel. I want to meet people. I want to see the world. I want to do all of that." That was probably the defining moment, looking back at it.

Before going to college in Shannon, I had some practical experience in the pub at home, although the pub was no longer my aunt's but belonged to Breda and Wolfgang Stromes. Coincidentally, Breda had gone to Shannon College. I had been working in the pub since my Inter Cert – in today's world, probably younger than I should have been, I'm sure!

The first thing you learn from working in pubs is that everybody is absolutely different – some of them are from a similar social background and interests to you and some of them are completely different, you might never have met people like them before in your life! You have to manage all those people, without them realising that they are being managed! You have to know when to listen, when to go away – but you also have to know when you've heard enough and when you don't want to hear any more. You learn to categorise them. There are maybe three general personalities: the nice friendly ones, the OK ones, and the ones that are not so nice and you need to watch out for. And then you have to manage them all individually. You learn that the counter is the border – you keep that counter between the customer and yourself all the time. I think that counter exists with you for the rest of your life in the hospitality business. It's always there – with your owner, with your colleagues, with your management, with your staff, with your customers – the counter is constant. That stops the over-familiarisation, the over-friendliness, the inappropriate comments. One of the trainers at the hotel school in Shannon used to say that, in order to be a barman, you had to be an acrobat, a diplomat, and a doorman. In the hotel business, it's exactly the same.

In order to get into Shannon College, you have to get work experience. I was probably 17 and about to do my Leaving Cert. I was at the wedding of my mum's sister Marian in the Strand Inn in Dunmore East when the owner, Mike Foyle, came over to talk to us at the table. I said I needed a job for the summer to get into college and that it sounded like fun, working there by the beach. So he kindly offered me a job for the summer. Again, I was behind the bar, which I was well used to from home, but this was a bigger bar so there were more personalities and more staff. It was wonderful.

All the staff – I suppose there were 10 or 12 of us, all students – had to 'live on'. What was interesting was that we weren't all studying or planning to study hotel management: some were becoming doctors, some were becoming lawyers, one even was becoming a priest! I remember thinking how good some of these people were at their job but yet they had no interest in the hospitality business. I thought, "I'm the only person here who actually wants to be a hotelier. And I want to run some of the finest hotels in the world. But that guy is actually better at doing this job than I am!". I think that improved my commitment and my dedication and prepared me for college. Mike and Edwina Foyle were great to learn from and they ran a very good ship. The Strand is run now by their son and daughter, Cliff and Louise, but under the watchful eye of their mother Edwina, I have no doubt. They do a great job and it's a great place where we still go on holidays.

The following September I started in Shannon. In those days, we lived in the airport hotel, which was closed to the public during the winter because there were so few flights coming in from America. We had this empty hotel that we ran as a 'play hotel', with third years as managers and first years as staff. The first years served breakfast, prepared the lunches and the evening meals through the college classes and the lectures. The head chef and the head housekeeper were all lecturers and, through the daily process, they ran a hotel staffed by the students – for the students!

The only downside was that nobody made your bed for you. You had to do that yourself. Your room had to be serviced every day and sometimes was checked by the head acting housekeeper. Needless to say, the rooms were never done properly and there was always World War III!

Punctuality was another feature of Shannon. Every morning, you would march down the corridor and Jorgen Blum, who was the Swiss principal of the college, like a hotel manager, sergeant major and headmaster merged into one, would stand on the corridor. If you weren't five minutes early going to class, then you were in big trouble because it would take you five minutes to get into your seat, get sitting down and ready for lectures. It was an incredibly different experience than being in an ordinary college.

We didn't have a lot of freedom, we didn't have a lot of independence, everything was very, very structured. I guess two things happened to people: they either flipped and said, "This ain't for me" or they lived with the regime. I found that I brought those principles with me and they were my principles when I came to run a hotel. They taught me the discipline of how a hotel should be run, how the customer should be treated and how the staff should interact and all of that. I suppose it created the theatre: the stage when I'm on show and when I'm not. The walking down the corridor to get to the lecture was our 'on show'; the scramble in your room to get ready was the behind-the-scenes. But you still presented yourself immaculately, looking like a million dollars. In the hotel business, sometimes you could be up till 4 o'clock in the morning but you still present yourself immaculately at 8 o'clock, because it's not the customers' concern what problems you have been dealing with behind the scenes.

Shannon was a great experience – the lectures and training, especially under masters at the business like Hans Schmid and the other staff, were important and wonderful but the best part was the Swiss experience. I worked in Zurich on the Bahnstrasse. I shared a horrible room above the restaurant complex with two others. We started as chefs in the kitchen, but because we couldn't speak or read any German we couldn't read the roster. So we were all late for work the first morning. Worse, even if we had been on time, we would still have been late because, in Switzerland, if you're starting at 8.30, you must clock in at about 8. And in German, "8.30" translates as "half nine" but they mean half an hour before 9 o'clock! So, on our first day, already we had the CEO of the place shouting and roaring at us! But life carries on. We muddled our way through it and learnt to speak 'work Swiss-German' very quickly!

But it was great and then we learnt an awful lot. I think the biggest take-out ever in terms of the hotel business and certainly what stayed with me was control. We worked in an incredibly busy unit with four or five restaurants, 2,500 covers, on the Bahnstrasse. To replace the bond system where the waiters worked independently and had their own cash register, around their waist essentially, the company decided to implement a computer system. Ours was the test site because it had the biggest food and beverage turnover. But the entire workforce worked against the computer system because it was going to destroy all of their petty theft and pilferage. By accident, myself and another colleague were put in charge of control. We only gave over the food when we had the ticket in our hand, and those tickets were what created the bill for those waiters – so we were the 'fiddle point'. We either stepped over the line and joined them or remained honest and trustworthy and did our job. It was probably fortunate that two of us were there at the same time because it was very, very difficult for a while. Management never stepped up to support us. One night the whole system crashed, which meant that the staff had access to absolutely everything and there was a free for all! That night my colleague and I looked at one another and said, "What do we do now?". "Guess we just write everything down" and that's what we did, we wrote everything down. At the end of the evening when the waiters were all called to cash up, we had a manual record of everything. You could see these guys thinking, "We thought we were going to take all this money home this evening"! We kept the line – that was a huge lesson in life for a trainee. And because in the 1980s they were putting in these computers, I figured, "They're investing millions in this, the multiples must be huge! Control must be important".

I also learnt lots of lessons about management support, what management should be doing and what not doing, which I suppose is the purpose of becoming a trainee manager. I guess we learnt nearly every trick in the book.

After Zurich, it was back to Shannon for the third year, which was very good – it was the academic year. I came back to work in Ireland in the summer, so there was a bit of a soft reintroduction. I went to Dundalk, to Ballymascanlon House Hotel, which owned by the Quinn family – the third generation is now running it. That was very interesting at the time – the Border was up the road and I was from Cashel, County Tipperary, and I had never been anywhere near the Border before! It was a busy summer. Ballymascanlon used to do a wedding nearly every day bar Sunday, five or six a week. I spent my entire time setting up the banqueting room in the morning, striking the tables, putting on the cloths, putting down the cutlery, getting out the jugs of water, doing the whole thing. Then the team would arrive and do the function and I'd clear it up and start again the next day!

It was great fun at Ballymascanlon. I will always remember a guest who was having dinner there one time. He ordered rack of lamb from the menu. When the lamb was served, it was pink and had a piece of thyme on it. He called me over and said, "Excuse me, young fellow, this sheep got caught in the ditch and it's still bleeding and has some of the ditch still stuck to it. Will you take it back please and have it killed, then cooked?". It was fun but it was hard work.

In Shannon, it was back into the discipline very quickly. Of course, we weren't the juniors in the college now, we were into third year and it flew because we were studying. I remember some people had to try hard and some didn't. I hadn't done accountancy or any business subjects for my Leaving Cert – so I remember that year as being a big catch-up. I was helped through it by some friends who were way ahead; they'd done it before and found it easy. There was the usual: somebody explaining "debits by the windows and credits by the door" and I wondered why they didn't just explain what a debit and a credit was, instead of this carry-on about where they go! Then I came out into work and suddenly the light bulb went on about what I had learnt academically.

In 2007, following the Ryder Cup at The K Club, I was invited by Phillip Smyth, Director of Shannon College, to be

Class Patron for the graduating year, which was a wonderful honour – something I never could have imagined when I was a student of the college. I graduated in 1998 and two of my three brothers, Donagh and Bryan, followed in my footsteps and studied at and are graduates of Shannon College of Hotel Management. Bryan's wife, Siobhan, and my cousin Jodie, are also graduates of the college. It's an outstanding college that absolutely provides the recipe and ingredients for success in this business.

In fourth year, I went to TrustHouseForte in the UK, which nearly everybody in Shannon did at the time. I was sent to Sheffield. Everyone said, "Oh, what are you going there for? It's a horrible place". But I always remember coming in on the train through the dip, through the whole industrial area, and then rising out of the city and into the suburbs and thinking, "Hey, this is a really nice place". It was a great experience. The general manager was George Cohen, who was a very well-known GM. He now runs The Saxton in Johannesburg in South Africa. He was very good, the sort of manager that stayed with you.

The first thing George did was to bring me into his office. "Sit down. I'm South African. You're from Ireland. So we're going to have tea. I'm going to show you how to pour a cup of tea in England because you do it completely different from how they do it here and all you Irish make the same mistake. And they'll make a laugh out of you over it. So you're not going to make that mistake". He had an affinity for the Irish, because he'd worked with a lot of them as a trainee himself. In those days, in England, as an Irishman, you could be the butt of a lot of jokes and you knew when you walked into a room that they were worried about terrorists strolling in too. "Would you like some milk?". When I said, "Yes", he said, "Milk first, then the tea". So that was a lesson learnt.

When we got over the tea, he told me what was going to happen and what I was going to do. He was an in-at-the-deep-end guy, very funny, very good and always very conscious of reporting to head office. The biggest lesson you learnt in TrustHouseForte at the time was that – this is pre-computers – they had their board reports on the entire company every Friday morning by 11 o'clock, which was all of the trading for all of their 800 hotels. That could only happen because of the discipline of every single hotel reporting on time. That discipline I think was the strongest thing I saw and, for the manager reporting those numbers, they were his bottom line. That was how THF was managed.

George Cohen was excellent. He was well-connected, so my first job as Assistant Manager was in a brand new Forte hotel in Hull that had just opened. I was 23 at most, in a brand new hotel, with 110 rooms. But it was in Hull – across the road were the fishermen coming off the boats, the market, factories and warehouses, and fish production places and derelict warehouses on the quays – the hotel was ahead of the curve at the time. A lot of people used to stay there from the oil and gas rigs off the North Sea. I remember the GM saying, "The best thing here is we're not close enough to Scotland so we're not a Scottish visit and we're way too far from Slough, so we never get head office visiting here. It's a great place to work!". Actually, it *was* a great place to work.

Forte had a great training system that was mostly geared around financial reporting. The first implementation of their property management system happened while I was there so I remember that very well. It was a massive training initiative across the company. When I was there about a year and a half, I was at a monthly financial review with the Area Director and Peter Vincent, the GM. The Area Director at the time, who was Irish, was going through the figures and said, "Davern's beverage revenue is behind 5% on last year in the first quarter. Why?". I said, "Well, it's interesting you should ask that. We can't really find a reason …" and he interrupted, "Oh, you can't find a reason? Do you think it's good enough to come to this meeting without a reason?". I said, "Well … what I was going to say is that we can't find a reason but we're assuming it's because, in the first quarter, there's a novelty factor. People are interested in the new hotel, so they come in and they buy a beer to have a look around. So there's a spike in the beverage turnover compared to covers, compared to sleepers, but not in the second year when they have already had a look around". He said, "All right. Did you just come up with that now?". I said, "No, but that's the only reason I can think of. There must be more like us somewhere that have had the same experience". He turned to the guy beside him, a financial guy, and said, "Do you know the answer to that?". He looked it up and started to pull out some numbers for the other hotels and then said, "There might be some logic to that, yeah. We'll have to check a few other new openings".

When the meeting finished and we were all getting up, the Area Director said, "Michael, would you just stay behind please?" and I always remember the GM put his hand on my shoulder as if to say, "Good luck. God help you". When they left, the Area Director asked me my age and I explained that I was 24. He said, "Do you realise that you are not going to get much further because nobody gets a senior position here until they are probably 29, turning 30. You're not going to move through the ladder here until then. You would be better off to go somewhere else – don't burn any bridges – and to come back to the company in about five years' time and pick up from where you left off with some other experience and you'll be catapulted into your next position". I remember leaving the meeting, going into the office and picking up the *Caterer & Hotelkeeper* magazine to see what jobs were available.

I saw a job in Sheffield for a company that I knew called Fretwell Downing, which did computer installations for cost control for catering environments. There were no computers when I was in school or in college so I wasn't the cleverest guy in the world with them. I figured that maybe this was an opportunity to use that time wisely, to catch up on computers and to figure out how they worked. So I applied for the job and became an Assistant Project Manager for computer installations. At the time, Fretwell Downing was mostly dealing with the National Health Service's kitchens in all the hospitals, providing patient and staff catering, as well as school meals services, and catering for the police and the fire service. They were basically going in and computerising mass production units that I hadn't even realised existed. The job was initially more or less data entry – there's a carrot, they come in pounds and they cost 10 pence a pound, put that in the computer. Then we went to implement these systems. I can't remember which was my first project but I remember Cambridge CookFreeze as a project I spent a lot of time on. I think it produced over 100,000 meals a day, for schools, hospitals and the fire service. The Queen Elizabeth II hospital, outside London, was another project. It was production planning, manning, management, procurement, cost control, all done through computers.

I suppose it was a brave step, to move outside the hotel business to learn. But there was an Area Director, a very successful gentleman giving very sound advice and computerisation and technology was literally just arriving and I knew I'd missed the start of it. I looked around the industry and I saw guys doing my job who were a lot older than me, so I thought, "If I'm going to kick some time around, this is the time to do it". So it was the right move, at the right time, and I went and I did it.

I was promoted to Senior Project Manager at Fretwell Downing and I spent probably three years with that company. At the later stage, we were project managing the installations and consulting for Granada Motorway Services, which was very interesting. I learnt a lot, but got to the point where I absolutely hated driving to get to a job in Aberdeen or wherever.

Around then, the UK went into a terrible economic crash, so I was in a technology company that was installing into all these places and the foot started to go on the brake for a lot of these companies. They were running out of budget or they were re-applying their budget somewhere else. There were redundancies and retrenchments starting in the company and, while my section was fine, that was a defining moment. I remember thinking, "I'll go back into hotels".

I went home to Tipperary for a holiday. At the time, Ray Carroll had just bought The Cashel Palace Hotel. He was a predecessor of mine here at The K Club – in fact, he opened

The K Club in 1991. I asked about his background and was told, "He's Sandy Lane, Barbados, and Grosvenor House, London". I knew The Grosvenor House well, so I thought, "That's interesting. I need to start to get on with my hotel experience." So I started to think about going somewhere overseas – not the UK, but further afield. The Caribbean or America were big on my mind at the time but maybe a week later somebody told me about a new project in Ireland – an absolutely wonderful five star resort being built by a famous Irish businessman and millionaire called Michael Smurfit – and I remember thinking, "That's sounds like an exciting place. I could get some great experience there. I just need five star experience now. If I can just get it at any level, then I can jump overseas". I made some inquiries and was told that the consultant in charge of the project was actually Ray Carroll and that he was in charge of recruiting. So I wrote to him, and was asked to come and meet him. He said, "Look, we have hired everybody at management level for The K Club". I said, "That's fine, I don't need a job as a manager, I just want to work there". "Where do you want to work?" and I said, "I just need five star experience. An opening like this, I just need it on my CV". He said, "There's only one job we haven't filled: night manager". "No", I said, "Anything but that. I'd meet no one, no one would see or meet me. It would be totally counter-productive for me. I need to be there during the day, to see what's happening. I need to see the skill level and to learn the five star luxury operation. I need to see what the others are bringing to the table. It's all about that experience". "Well, I don't think I have anything else but if something comes up, I will let you know." End of interview.

But about a week or so later, when I was back at work in the UK, there was a phone call for me: "A gentleman called Ray

Carroll looking for you". Ray said, "We realise that we need somebody who understands a bit about computers. We're doing an awful lot of purchasing here and I need a controller. You've a lot of experience in computers, maybe you could come on board?" So that's how I came here to The K Club.

As you can imagine with any opening, but particularly here, there was box-loads of stuff arriving from all over: cutlery and china, silverware, soaps, shampoos, antiques, paint, wallpapers, carpets, curtains and golf course machinery. The K Club opened in July 1991; when I came here in April the builders were still in the hotel, finishing off. It was at interior design and fit-out stage, and the Palmer club house was almost finished. It was a very exciting project at that time: Ireland's first world-class hotel with AA Five Red Star status and Michelin star ambition. There was a great young and dynamic team in place, creating standards never seen before in Ireland at that time. It was unprecedented but driven by Ireland's leading entrepreneur, who knew all about world-class.

From 1991 to 1997, I stayed in The K Club and held a number of managerial roles. I was Deputy General Manager looking after food and beverage from probably 1995 until I left in 1997.

I went to America on my holidays in 1994 with Aideen, who was my girlfriend at the time, and later became my wife. In America, I was looking around and thinking, "Is this the place I should try and get a job?". Nothing really motivated me enough at the time so the next year, we went on holidays to South Africa. I absolutely loved South Africa. I thought it was a fantastic place. While in the US, South Africa or any other country, I was always curious, always visiting hotels, visiting resorts, seeing new places. Travel is the university of life and certainly so in our business. Resorts were still new to me because Ireland was all hotels except for The K Club. When the next holiday came around, I thought, "Let's go back to South Africa".

On holidays in South Africa, I visited a resort called the Fancourt Hotel & Country Club Estate because Maura Nolan, a travel agent who I knew very well from America, had said to me, "If you're going to South Africa, there's a place there, very similar to The K Club, with great golf, called Fancourt, a great five star resort. It's owned by a very wealthy family from Germany who recently bought it". I said, "OK, great" and put it on my list. It was on the Garden Route and when we saw it, we decided we'd stay there. So we stayed in Fancourt, played a game of golf, and it was all just incredible value for money! I saw the whole potential of Fancourt, a magnificent place, and I always remember thinking, "This is how golf resorts work and I would love to manage such a place". I developed an affinity scheme with Fancourt and arranged for The K Club members to visit and *vice versa*.

In probably January or February 1997, I was thinking, "I'm not going anywhere else in The K Club right now. So what's the next move?" so I started to investigate a bit. I was lucky enough to have a conversation with Dermot Desmond, who together with his business partners had just bought Sandy Lane in Barbados. I thought, "That's an iconic place, I'd love to work there". Mr. Desmond put me in touch with Richard Williams, the CEO of Sandy Lane at the time, and we began to discuss opportunities. But it was not to be as then I got a phone call from a gentleman I'd met in Fancourt, Gavin McCann, who was selling real estate there. He said, "They're looking for a general manager. I want to put your name forward". Apparently, the estate had had nine general managers since the new owners in Germany had bought it. Gavin said, "None of them get it. The owner just wants it a certain way. And I can't sell real estate while this carries on. We need to sort it! I want to put you forward". I said, "OK, that'd be great".

I got a call to go to Germany because the owner of Fancourt wanted to meet with me. This was around Easter, late March, I think. I jumped on a plane from Dublin to Frankfurt – I remember it cost a fortune at the time. I had been told that there was a hotel such-and-such and "If you stay at that hotel, this gentleman named Hasso Plattner will meet you there because that hotel is near his office". I got on the plane, went to Frankfurt and figured my way from Frankfurt airport to Heidelberg. I got to the hotel, where they had lost my reservation and had no messages waiting for me. I didn't know what time was I meeting Dr. Plattner and I couldn't get hold of anyone – no mobile phones, no email in those times. So the next morning, I was down in the lobby about 8.30, ready for my meeting.

Well past 10.30, the doors opened in a hurry and a lady and gentleman – Hasso Plattner and his wife, Sabine – came in and there was a bit of hullaballoo. "Ah, OK. Hello. Chaos, don't know what happened. We thought you didn't even arrive!". They kindly had arranged a car for me the previous evening and, of course, they thought I had not shown.

We sat down at a table where there were hour-old teas and coffees. I just couldn't stomach the sight of them so I said, "Excuse me" and lifted up the teas and coffees and put them on another table, just clearing the table. I started to tell him about The K Club. We talked about where I had worked and then he was talking about hotels and golf and the market and five star luxury. Then he asked, "What makes you think you can go to South Africa and run a hotel? It's so difficult. It's all unions and culture and environment and apartheid". I said, "I have been to South Africa twice on holidays. I loved the place. I think it's fantastic. I have been to Fancourt ...". We were warming up and he was liking it. I went on, "I have absolutely no baggage. I know nothing about apartheid. I never visited South Africa during apartheid. I'm Irish. We have a natural affinity towards people. All I would do is manage the property as best I possibly could with the people that are there and train them and improve them to deliver good service levels". He said, "Yeah, no baggage, I like that".

Next he said, "I have to go soon. I'm late for another meeting". He said to Mrs. Plattner that he couldn't spend any more time so he would bring me back to the office, talk to me in the car and I could go to the airport from the office. So I grabbed my bag and we went out and got into a black Porsche. About five minutes away, we pulled up right at the front door of one of two huge tall buildings with SAP signage. He parked the car right at the front door where there was a big sign saying 'No Parking'. As I got out of the car, I said, "I don't think you're supposed to park here. It says, 'No Parking'". He looked at me and burst out laughing, "The Irish! You have a great sense of humour!".

He walked into the building and immediately people looked at him and there was an air that someone very respected had walked in. Everyone greeted him, saying, "Good afternoon, Dr. Plattner". I hadn't realised that here was the visionary, the founder of this massive IT company. In hindsight, I think it was probably like walking into the Microsoft building with Bill Gates!

I asked Dr. Plattner what the company did and he explained about SAP and offered to get me a brochure. "Oh, I used to work for a computer company". "You never told me you worked for a computer company. What did you do?" I explained and he said, clapping his hands, "That's good. I did not see that on your CV so I think you might be the man for the job!". Dr. Plattner arranged a lift for me to the airport and I flew home.

The next morning at about 7 o'clock I got a phone call at my house. It was a lady named Ingrid Diesel from South Africa, who was running the development company for the Plattners at the Fancourt estate, ringing to say my interview with the Plattners had gone well. "I'll fax you through an offer and a contract. And we'd really love you to start as soon as possible." I remember thinking, "What a challenge!". I was 29 years of age and at 29 there was only one person in the world who would offer me a job running a hotel and resort that big and that was somebody in the software world who saw me like he saw a computer programmer – age or grey hair didn't matter, he just saw the person and their potential. I really liked his style. The challenges were to be enormous but the confidence shown in me by the Plattners always allowed me to take them on and Ingrid Diesel was always supportive.

Shortly after signing and sending back the Fancourt contract, I met Mr. Desmond. I told him that I was going to South Africa and he wished me luck, offered me his help if I ever needed it and said that perhaps one day I might work at Sandy Lane.

I headed off to South Africa in June 1997. It was mid-winter down there so the resort was very quiet. The first person I met there was Lawrence Gould, whose nickname was 'Polyfilla'. He was 'Polyfilla' because it was something like his sixth stint in a row minding Fancourt while it waited for another general manager! I remember well arriving at George airport, where Lawrence was there to meet me. I figured out quickly that I was only ever going to be in charge when Lawrence had gone because only then could I stand on my own two feet and begin to earn the respect I needed. So we played golf, had a few beers and some dinner while we chatted and handed over and Lawrence left a day or so later.

I remember sitting there thinking, "This is 900 staff, 1,200 acres, in the new South Africa, labour law is chaos, changing every day, the unions, all sorts of issues … this is literally going to make me or break me. I'm either going to be the next GM who failed to run Fancourt or I'm going to be the guy who succeeded in running what is one of the most serious challenges but also greatest resorts in the business. Where will I go at 30 years of age if I'm the guy who failed in Fancourt?". So I just got stuck into it. I was on my own down there – Aideen didn't come down until later – so I just lived and breathed Fancourt 24/7 for about six months. I got stuck into every single operation, discussion, argument or union meeting, every standards meeting, and every management issue.

But the first thing I had to do was to get the trust and confidence of the staff who had come from working in a hostile environment towards management. One of the staff's big issues was that all of the management were white and therefore they had no trust – and I was just another white guy. The owners were very supportive of the new South Africa: an affirmative action policy was in place but naturally it was not moving fast enough for the black and coloured staff. So I leant on the fact that I wasn't just another white guy, I was an *Irish* white guy!

The first thing I wanted to do was to introduce myself to all of the staff. The response was "Really? Introduce yourself? To all the staff? OK, there's 900 staff, so we'll organise that for Thursday, probably in the afternoon. The buses leave at 3 o'clock on the early shift and they arrive at 3 o'clock on the late shift but there's a half-an-hour window between … so we've got maybe 20 minutes if we start at 3.05 on Thursday where the buses can stall and we can get this done". That's what we did, in our Human Resource building where the Human Resource offices were, where the clinic was, where the nurses were, where the staff catering was, where the delivery trucks used to come in under the ground and go on up to the hotel – it was bigger than most hotels and certainly like nothing I had ever seen before!

Timothy Ndwani was the Assistant Director of Human Resource and I had very quickly figured out that Timothy was strategically a very important man for me. So Timothy was chosen to introduce me. I started speaking and introduced myself and Timothy translated what I said. And then he translated again and then again and when he had finished, I said, "Timothy, I said just one sentence". He replied, "But I have to translate into Xhosa, Afrikaans and the other official languages". I said, "Seriously?" and he said, "Yes". Besides the realisation that this was going to be different and challenging, Timothy could be saying anything at all and what would I have known! We joked about it and everyone enjoyed that.

I knew the caddies were an important part of the team, so the following day I went to meet them, about 80 of them. At about 9 o'clock I said I was going to see the caddies before they went out because I had heard that they were going to go filling divots at 10 o'clock. I went into the area beyond the Human Resource building where the caddies had assembled and I immediately felt a semi-hostile environment. I'd played golf at Fancourt a couple of times when I'd been on holidays and I knew a couple of faces and names, so I asked one of the guys I recognised to introduce me. He called them all up, "Let the boss speak! Let's hear what he has to say!". I thought, "I just wanted to say 'Hello' and now it's like a political address". As I started to speak, the door opened and some security guards came in to check if I was secure. I understood quickly that a white guy like me generally did not visit the caddies and could feel threatened. But we began to build a relationship from there that was based on respect and trust for their important role in our overall team. After all, who else spends as much time with the guests as the caddies?

After that, everything was just about being firm, fair, applying the rules and regulations. But every day was a game, with staff twisting the rules and trying to create issues and problems, trying to promote their own colour or race. Every disciplinary action was like a Privy Council hearing with representatives everywhere. The whole aim was to deconstruct the entire process, to make it fall apart – everything was a threat towards another strike with no trust built up. I wanted to avoid a strike, come hell or high water – the owner wanted to avoid another strike also. So I just had to manage my way through it step by step and build up trust.

After the first six months, things seemed to begin to work out and we had started a lot of training and development. And once the team saw that I was genuinely going to pass on knowledge, suddenly they were the greatest people you ever could have the pleasure of working with. These people were starved of knowledge, of empowerment, of information, of training – and they became great friends and allies.

After I had been at Fancourt for a few months, Aideen came down. She had a lot of experience in the hotel business because she had been Front Office Manager and Head Receptionist in The K Club – that's where I met her first. When she came down to South Africa, the owners, Dr. and Mrs. Plattner, said it was absolutely crazy not to have this talent working on training the staff so she became Front of House manager and worked under a South African senior manager. She did a lot of training in front of house skills, and did a wonderful job. I hired a great Scottish Director of Golf, Elliott Gray, and there was a great South African Food & Beverage Manager, Elsje Balzun. I built a team around me who worked extremely hard to earn the international recognition that Fancourt and its staff and shareholders deserved. I hired people who were on the same wavelength as myself or brought them there – no baggage, completely open-minded, open to wanting to train, open to change – and that's what we got, a lot of really good people. A lot of people got promoted through the system – and a lot of people fell out along the journey too.

One of the outstanding issues that I remember was the first disciplining and dismissal of a white manager. I didn't see it as an issue: the person in question had screwed up, due process was followed, and the person had gone through the same process as everybody else. But I suppose what I didn't really realise was that, in their heart of hearts, the staff constantly believed that, as soon as the issue would get to me at GM level, I'd find an excuse to throw it out and protect the white manager. Why would they think otherwise, because that's what would have always occurred in the past? In the end, the person lost their job. That day, there was almost euphoria amongst the workers because a white person was fired. It was a massive turning point. Unfortunately, it had to be done and dismissing somebody, which is never easy, had to be done in that case because it was the right thing to do no matter what their position, race or creed.

I was in Fancourt for just under five years – actually four years and 10 months. It was a long chapter in my life but a wonderful one with great experiences. You can imagine the behind-the-scenes but, on the positive side, we constructed three golf courses and renovated the resort, the property flourished, and we hosted the Commonwealth Heads of Government retreat – that, in itself, was a year's undertaking. It was wonderful for the whole team, who suddenly were looking after 54 presidents and prime ministers. It was huge for the country, huge for the government, and very important for the owners. The entire team also got to meet Nelson Mandela, who came to visit them with his wife, Graça Machel.

That was my stand-out day for me in the hotel business: greeting Nelson Mandela at the front door of the hotel at Fancourt. I can't remember the exact date but Nelson Mandela and his wife decided to come and stay at the hotel before the Commonwealth Heads of Government retreat for a purely restful weekend. Obviously a huge amount of planning kicked into that because he was coming but there also was a tremendous excitement that we had to keep a lid on. The employees felt they owned Nelson Mandela – this iconic man is coming to visit and why wouldn't they shake his hand? I remember we thought about it very carefully and it was decided to ask if he could take some time out to meet and greet all of the staff. He agreed, which was wonderful. I knew it was not really my role to welcome him. I was the Irish guy, a white guy, who happened to be the General Manager running the place. So it was decided that the best person to represent the employees would be somebody from Human Resource and the obvious person was our Assistant Human Resource Director, Timothy Ndwani, from the Xhosa tribe – Mandela's tribe. But, as the black BMW Seven Series car containing Nelson Mandela pulled up, Timothy's knees literally went from under him, he started to cry and went to walk away. Nelson Mandela got out of the car, saw what was happening and immediately walked through the small crowd of people. He grabbed Timothy and hugged him as if he was his brother who had got bad news and, when he had calmed him, said, "It's fine", shook his hand, asked him who he was and spoke with him as we all walked into the lobby. The hair literally stood up on the back on my neck. Later, I was lucky enough to sit for lunch with Nelson Mandela ('Madiba' as he was known in South Africa) and Graça Machel.

It's never ever important to me that I have to be the person meeting a VIP. If it's important that they meet the General Manager, then it's important that they do – but I'm only a figurehead. The VIP didn't come to meet me; that's just not what we do as GMs. The hotel is about the people, the team, the staff – never about the General Manager.

Towards the end of my time at Fancourt, just prior to coming home for holidays and to get married, a headhunter called me and asked me if I was interested in a position in Dubai. I remember thinking, "I'm going home on holidays. It's about time I started getting my skates on to leave South Africa.

I must put the word out now that I'm going to move and see what happens". So I did. I told two or three people whom I knew had very good contacts – and what came back was so positive that, before I came home for holidays I felt the time was nearing to leave South Africa, go home to get married and to look at where I was going next.

I met with Mr. Desmond at his office in Dublin a few days before getting married and that was that. I went to Sandy Lane as General Manager of Sandy Lane Properties and Golf, which was developing the two golf courses and the real estate and so on at the time. I worked alongside Richard Williams, the CEO of Sandy Lane, who was in his final months before retiring.

I had been exposed a fair amount to golf construction because we'd built three golf courses in Fancourt with Gary Player. I had a lot of golf experience from The K Club and Fancourt. I knew a lot of people in golf and could speak their language.

My job initially was like an owner's representative's role: somebody to translate, or try to translate, the owner's vision and make sure the designer and the construction team delivered on it. For any hotelier to gain experience of construction at this level, pre-opening, is a great learning curve and invaluable experience. Little did I realise five years earlier when I decided to go to Fancourt that Sandy Lane would be on the cards for me and I had learnt so much more in the meantime.

Sandy Lane was a wonderful experience and every hotelier's dream. I was there to see the last Concorde flight wave goodbye along the beach line, tipping its wings. To be on the opening team of one of the world's most famous and iconic hotels and furthermore under the ownership of some of Ireland's most respected entrepreneurs and businessmen was not only a privilege but a dream come true.

I left Sandy Lane in September 2005, after almost five years, to come back to The K Club a year before it was to stage the Ryder Cup. At the time, Dr. Smurfit was negotiating to buy The K Club, which was then owned by the private equity firm, Madison Dearborn Capital Partners. The CEO of The K Club, Ray Carroll, was retiring and I got a call from Gary McGann, CEO of Smurfit Group, to take up the position at The K Club. Mr. Desmond was very supportive and proud that I was going to return to The K Club to oversee the Ryder Cup, which would be the largest sporting event ever hosted in Ireland.

The Ryder Cup team and European Tour people know what they are doing. It's a big machine, it's a well-oiled machine. They take over the site and roll out the infrastructure. But there's a huge amount of preparation work and planning that has to go into it also: liaising with them, liaising with the Gardaí (the Irish police), the owners, and the stakeholders. The number of stakeholders in something like the Ryder Cup is enormous and they extend beyond your expectation.

I guess the Commonwealth Heads of Government retreat was very helpful experience in terms of running a resort hosting the Ryder Cup. Along with running the Ernie Els Invitational in South Africa, I and my team at Fancourt had done all the planning for the President's Cup in South Africa, which is the next biggest tournament to The Ryder Cup and involved dealing with the PGA in America. And in my previous stint at The K Club, I had experienced three European Opens in a pretty hands-on role there. At Sandy Lane, we brought the World Cup of Golf to Barbados so I was very involved in the early planning although I wasn't there when it took place. All that previous experience helped me immensely with the Ryder Cup at The K Club.

The weather for the Ryder Cup was extremely poor and challenging – before and after was fabulous, but during was dreadful – but the show went on! The entire team here – and especially our green-keeping team under the leadership of Gerry Byrne – were incredibly challenged obviously, but it's all about the preparation. You don't get any better person checking on that preparation than somebody like Dr. Smurfit. His mantra was "prepare for the worst and hope for the best". With a massive event, whether it's the Commonwealth Heads of Government retreat or the Ryder Cup, you don't sit there and say, "If we're all really motivated, it'll all be great on the day". You write down every single thing that could possibly go wrong and figure out what you are going to do about each one when it happens on your watch. That's what it comes down to – identifying every single problem and then eliminating them one by one. If you can anticipate nearly everything, you'll be prepared – and we were.

I think success as a hotelier is a lot about self-discipline and dedication. You have to be observant, you have to have lots of common-sense, you have to be able to weigh up the problem, the opportunity or whatever it is going on around you and then you have to make a decision about how you are going to react to that situation.

If something is really important to you in your business, no matter who you are dealing with, whether you're dealing with staff, whether you're dealing with an owner, if it's really important, you have got to make sure that the answer is going to be "Yes" when you ask the question, not "No". Why pose the question when there's a 60 / 40 risk that the answer may be "No"? If you think the answer may be "No", go back and do your homework.

I learnt from Dr. Smurfit one great mantra – management is very simple: it's step 1, 2, 3, problem, solution, implementation. That's it, there's nothing more to it. Presented with a problem, analyse the facts, come up with a solution and then go and implement the solution. If you have decided on the solution, what are you doing hanging around? Go get it done. Move it on and then the next one will come along.

I know that many younger managers believe that their job is to present problems to the boss, for the boss to figure out. But I see the role of the manager actually to present the problem, to present the solution and then to ask whether you can implement the solution.

If you're a young person considering coming into the hotel industry and you're looking at people like me and thinking, "That's why I want to go into the hotel business", then you're looking at the wrong guy! There are very few resorts like this, compared to the number of hotels. If you want to go into the hotel business, then have a look at what the hotel business really is. It is really at the three star or four star level. It's about differentiating to sell bedrooms, to put heads on beds, every night. It's about driving occupancy, being warm, being friendly, being hospitable but it's not really looking for service levels that are extraordinary – the guests in many cases are looking for a comfortable bed and little more. Identifying what the customer truly values and delivering it; if the guest values it, then they will be happy to pay for it – that's the hotel business!

There's a huge amount of luck if you want to end up running a place like The K Club or Sandy Lane or Fancourt – so it should not be the key issue in deciding to join this industry. The key issue is that you have to enjoy the business of hotelkeeping – and today there is a huge amount to that business – liking people and travel is not enough. If you get into the hotel business and you like people, great – but if you want to get on in the hotel business, you need to be a good generalist as a manager because you are going to be managing finance, IT, people (both customers and staff), daily revenue systems, sales, marketing, distribution channels – and much more.

At the luxury end, the hotel business as we know it is going to change as guests look more and more for independent hotels that deliver a truly authentic experience. A manager who is looking for the company manual on the shelf with the answer to every problem in it is not going to be a success in the future because the industry is looking for people who can think on their feet, who can listen to the customer in their specific area in their specific market and figure out what ticks the boxes for that customer. What are my customers really looking for? And how do we deliver that?

When I make mistakes is when I don't get involved in the detail as much as I should because I think, "Maybe I shouldn't interfere" – but my job is to interfere! My job is to ask the team, specialists who often may know more about what they are doing than I do, "Why did you do it that way?", "Do you think that's right?", "How exactly are we going to deliver the required result?" and "How will we exceed the customer's expectation?". I make no apologies for it. Next to anybody on this team talking to and communicating with the shareholders on a daily basis, the person who owns the brand, manages the brand and looks after the brand's future and its reputation is me! It's my role for a relatively short period of time in the long history of a great property, so I'd better do it well!

At this level of business in The K Club or properties like this, particularly when you work for individual owners, you're managing their vision and what you think their dream is for the property. They didn't do it for any other reason – they had a vision or a dream and that's what you have to endeavour to identify and deliver on. They didn't just want to own a hotel; they wanted to create something very special, something very unique, something that suited them and the way they perceive their lifestyle. That 'something' fits into that hotel or resort and they know that there's like-minded people who want that and those people are who we are targeting as customers. So you're really translating all of that.

I have had the pleasure of working with Dr. Smurfit for a long time, when I was here initially and then very closely for the last 10 years or so, very closely indeed with the Ryder Cup, which was a very important moment for The K Club and for him also. He has been a pioneer in many ways for the hotel industry in Ireland. He created the first international five star resort in Ireland, and he brought the Ryder Cup to the country. He had the vision to do that, which comes from creating a world-class business because everything he wants to do is obviously world-class – his attention to detail is unbelievable. But attention to detail is what drives hoteliers anyway, because attention to detail is what our business is. It's what hotelkeeping is all about.

BERNARD MURPHY

Gleneagles Hotel, Scotland

Brands Hatch Racing Circuit
The Churchill Inter-Continental, London
The Britannia Inter-Continental, London
Compass Group
Gleneagles Hotel, Scotland

I didn't come here to work at the
second best hotel in Scotland.

I grew up in Kent, about 25 miles outside London. Nobody in my family had anything to do with the hotel business at all. My father was an engineer. My mother ultimately was a nurse, although she was at home while I was growing up. I had two brothers, both younger than me.

School was fine – I went through the 11+ exam and got into grammar school. Academically, I was out in front by a mile until about the age of 14 and then I started to find other things distracting. Thankfully, I had done enough by then not to worry. I didn't do any work for O levels but got them anyway – but A levels were harder because, frankly, I just didn't do anything.

We didn't have too much money as a family when I was growing up – I wouldn't want to paint it as being poverty-stricken or anything like that but, at the earliest opportunity, I got a proper weekend job. I'd always had paper rounds to get a few bob but, once you're 16, you can work officially. I managed to get a job in the catering team at Brands Hatch, the racing circuit, near to which we lived. I worked both days at the weekend from at least 8 am until 6 pm and, when I was 18, until later in the evening because I could then do bar work. None of this was overly helpful towards A levels and academia, but it meant I could buy a car and go to nightclubs and do all that sort of stuff which was appealing at the time!

And I think that was probably where it began. Work just seemed so much fun; I was working with the public, the fellow I was working for was really good, and I thought, "I wonder if this is what I should do".

Getting a job, being able to buy my own car, probably occupied an undue weighting in my psyche right the way through my teens. Then in the summer holidays – it was when the City privatisations were happening under Margaret

Thatcher – I did some temping in an insurance company, and they asked me to stay on. There's a bit of a parallel here: my father's parents tried to get him to work at the Prudential; he worked there for one day, came home, and took up an engineering apprenticeship. I can remember to this day my father asking, "Do you know what you're going to do?" and I said, "I'm not sure you're going to want to hear this but I want to go to university. I want to do the hotel thing. That's what I set out to do and just because these guys have offered me a job isn't a reason to change that". He was excellent. He just said, "You've made a decision. Well, that's what we're going to do then". It surprised me because I realised that financially there's an implication for your parents of you going to university.

I had decided in going to university that I would study hospitality. I think it came from that job at Brands Hatch actually. The manager there, Chris Rawlinson, who I still know and talk to today, now runs an event management company, but he sort of stumbled into this catering thing. I don't think he did much at school, I think he just wanted to get out and work. He was very young when he was manager at Brands Hatch, mid-20s at most. He was good fun because he wasn't really much older than I was, so we got the work done, got loads of work done, made money for the company, worked very hard but it was just fun.

Nothing was ever a problem to Chris; he just seemed to enjoy life. And I thought, "This is a career that's rewarding and lucrative" so I guess that shaped my A-level subject choices. I took French and German because I figured they might be useful. It's turned out that they have been no use at all in my career – they're handy when we go on holiday but that's about the extent of it because I can't do much more than order a cup of coffee in either language, not having spent enough time in either country.

I went to university at Portsmouth, then Portsmouth Polytechnic. Once I got there, I met up with just some fantastic people, made really good friends. I didn't have a great start to university, the accommodation was all wrong and all that sort of stuff – and it was my first time living away from home, too. One of the things I often say to people about their teenage children – my children are younger than that – is that who you are friendly with shapes where you get to. One of my teachers, at the point where I was on the way down and not paying attention, wrote about me in a school report, "A very capable and very amiable young man who is very poor at picking his classroom friends". I didn't care at the time – but I'd stand by that now. At university, four of us shared a house for three years; two of us got a first (the only two firsts on our course), the other two got an upper second degree. If I look at the circle of friends I had at school, they've not really done overly much; if I look at the circle of friends that I have extended through those university chums, they all have done very well in all sorts of different industries.

I went to work for Chris Rawlinson again during one of the university summers, because Brands Hatch built a hotel and Chris, who was the Food & Beverage Manager, basically just wanted to have a gopher to run around for him before the opening. That was interesting because the hotel got taken over by Thistle about three weeks before it was due to open. Brands Hatch did very well: they had spent £6m on it and sold it for something in the order of £13m before they even opened it, so that was all good news. But at the hotel, it was as if the life fell out of it overnight. It went from being what was going to be a really fun place to being just a building. The transformation was amazing – all these guys turned up from corporate and it was just different. It didn't make any difference to me because I was going back to university anyway. Don't get me wrong, I'm not anti-hotel companies *per se* but it just went that way there – and it went overnight. The leadership team changed and it wasn't the same; it was OK but it wasn't the same.

At university, I really enjoyed economics. I really enjoyed marketing. I could have ended up doing anything. It was funny, of 66 of us who graduated, only six went into the hotel business from our course because it was run from the business department at Portsmouth. Year three was in industry – it was more than a year, it was 15 months in point of fact because it was June to the following September when you went back. I really lucked out here with a placement at The Churchill Hotel in London. I think I got into around 12 departments in the year. It was a stellar placement, absolutely, in a five star hotel, with 450 rooms – it was just great.

Coming from where I came from, it's not like I travelled much internationally as a child or anything so suddenly I was in a hotel where 30% of the business was from the Middle East, 30% was from North America, we had about 10% from Greece – I never quite understood why that was – and then all-comers. Being a Brit and in an environment where there were almost no Brits – there was Portuguese staff, there was staff from India, from all over – I found that just like another world.

I remember the very first day I was in reception. The Resident Manager there – I don't quite know how he afforded it – was all Savile Row suits. He was just the best-dressed person I had ever seen in my whole life. He was standing in the front hall when I came out of the back office, and I was just petrified, walking across this lobby that just glistened, thinking, "I don't know if I belong here". But within two weeks or a month, I was thinking, "This where I belong. This is what I do. I know what I am doing". It's amazing how quickly you pick things up.

That Resident Manager taught me to read people and situations. He could see a situation coming a mile away. Sometimes he used to verbalise that while I was standing next to him. Other times, he'd bark things like, "Never turn your back on a guest at the reception desk, don't ever do that". He was old school, it was all about detail with him, and although I wasn't too sure of his approach at times I thought, "OK, he's standing up for standards here actually. That's important".

I left there at the end of my year and thought, "I need to do something different, so I'm going to go and work for three months of the summer down in a sea-side hotel". So The Grand Hotel in Eastbourne put me in the bar, where I lasted one week. The bar was very quiet and, to me, the staff accommodation seemed oriented around drinking and fighting. I rang up the Reception Manager at The Churchill and said, "Look, I only left a week ago. I've made just the most awful error here. Is there anything you can do for me for the next three months?" and he said, "Yeah, fine. Come back. Start Monday". Interestingly Chris Rawlinson, the catering manager at Brands Hatch, when I told him I wanted to work in hotels, he had said, "OK, if you really insist on doing it, and I think you're making a dreadful mistake by the way, stay at the top end. Stay in five star. Don't get drawn into anything else". As I left Eastbourne and went back to London, I remembered this piece of advice I had been given several years earlier! Things trigger with you after the event sometimes – not before!

I think my ambition or direction came from my wanting to 'get on'. I probably should have tried much harder to work internationally than I did and part of the reason for not doing so was always wanting to make sure that I got on the next rung. People said, "If you're not a GM by the time you're 30 or 35, you're not going to be". I didn't leave university and start work until I was nearly 23 so I felt I really had to get on with it and get moving. For that, I was prepared to work very, very hard. Paul Heery, our General Manager, and I do a double act at induction here. All the youngsters ask, "How do I get your job? How do I get to be a GM?". The short answer I give most of them, which they don't want to hear, is, "Hard work and endeavour. There are no short cuts". And, of course, all these Gen Y guys think, "There must be. There's a short cut for everything in life. There must be an app!" and so some of them nearly want to leave the room when they realise they're going to have to do this the hard way.

After graduation, I flirted with some of the insurance companies, largely because my friends were all going into finance and things like that and I thought, "I'll have a look". But I had a job offer from when I left The Churchill after my placement. They had said, "Come back. We'll find a job for you or we'll create a management trainee post for you" and that was quite nice to be walking around with a job in your back pocket in your final year in university – particularly since the year I graduated was when the first Iraq war broke out and tourism died. In the end, that's what I did. I went back to The Churchill and they had me as a Duty Manager, which was a fair responsibility actually at 23 for that sort of hotel. Because they promoted me to Front Desk Manager around a few people who had been there a lot longer, there was the inevitable, "Why is he getting it?". But the Rooms Division

Manager said, "Because he fixes stuff. He gets stuff done. He doesn't just turn up and look after guests all day. He does that – but he does more". We used to have all sorts of rate discrepancies from tour operators in those days. They were all kept in a shoebox and no one wanted to look at the shoebox. But I used to stay for a couple of hours after my shift ended and I would get some of that stuff moved on. And that's what I share with young people now: you've got to do more than the job description whereas many people are very oriented around, "Well, if that's the four things I've got to do, and if I do those four things, that should be enough because that's what you asked me to do". Of course, it doesn't work that way. I believe that you need to interpret what needs to be done and put a bit more of yourself in. Endeavour goes a very long way in the hotel business – it's an industry where hard work is entirely measurable.

There was a Banqueting Manager at The Churchill called George Brown, who said to me when I came back, "Good to see you back. You're the best student we ever had". I said, "Thank you, that's a very kind thing to say" and he said, "I'm not saying it, it's true. I'm glad you're on as a Duty Manager because at least the place will be run properly".

At The Churchill, we got some funny things to deal with. Now when we have crises, I look back on some of the things there. One morning we were having the President of an African nation come to stay. We also had the then US Secretary of State for Foreign Affairs coming the same day. The Americans used to take a whole floor for their principal, dogs in the lobby, all the routine. I got in early about 6.30 in the morning to start at 7 o'clock. Somebody phoned up and said they had left a bomb in our car park underneath the hotel. We got the police in and I stood there with the fellow from the Met and said, "What do we do here? These two VIPs, with their security, are coming in this morning". He said, "They didn't leave a code word, so I don't know. It's probably a hoax – but it's your hotel, your decision". I was 23 or 24 at the time, the senior manager – the only manager – on duty. In the end, we elected not to evacuate, and nothing happened. So that was the start of the morning. The GM got in about 8 o'clock and it was "Let's get on with the day".

Then the US Secretary of State turned up, got out of the car, a bulletproof car with the American outriders, walked into the lobby, with the American Secret Service holding the lift. Straight in behind him, unannounced, with no outriders, the African President turned up. He was supposed to arrive later, but he here he was. He bounced out of the car, no protection, just straight in through the front door like anybody else. Because he was a President, diplomatic protocol dictates that he had priority, so the Secretary of State shook his hand, dead surprised to see him here, since no one had briefed him he was going to be in the same hotel at the same time. Of course, the Secretary of State said, "You take the lift". The Secret Service guys went berserk because they've now got their principal stood still in the middle of a hotel lobby with no lift! This went on for probably two to three minutes – it seemed like an hour and a half. I remember I had to go back to my office afterwards for a cup of tea and a biscuit! "What else is going to happen today?" I don't think it was 9.30 yet! It was a really surreal morning.

We did evacuate The Churchill once. We had some pilots staying with us in one of our ninth floor suites. Pilots have these quite big briefcases, and one of them had left his out on a balcony. The room maid had seen it out on the balcony and quite rightly reported it. I went up, looked at it and thought,

"Why would somebody leave something like that on a balcony?" so we evacuated the hotel. The guest came back from shopping a couple of hours later – no apology at all – completely unaware of the chaos he'd caused. It was an awful morning for our guests, because we were out for a couple of hours, not just 10 minutes like a fire drill. Not a funny day.

I was at The Churchill when it was taken over by InterContinental. All the executive team went within the week, with the exception of me – they chose to keep me on. My then boss, the Resident Manager, had done me a bit of a favour. He had said, "You've got a young man there who's sufficiently malleable to your company. He'll devour your systems. He's highly intelligent. What you hire will no better than him. You should have a look", so they did. It was a difficult time because all of my colleagues were gone. They parachuted in a gentleman who was then their Vice President for Europe, Middle East and Africa, John Wright, who was a very severe man, very strict. I think he quite liked me because numerically I could keep up. He got wound up by people who couldn't keep up commercially, so he used to keep asking me questions about pick up rates and occupancies until he thought I got one wrong or until he got bored asking the questions. It was almost if you could get to question number eight, life was good, you'd passed the test, because most people would fail.

John was going to bed the property down for six months for InterContinental before they got a GM in to run it. I really enjoyed that time because you'd never get to work for a VP for Europe, Middle East and Africa in a single unit. He used to say, "We're harsh, but not brutal" – or maybe it was the other way around? "We're entitled to ride you very hard, but it needs to be fair" was what he was trying to say, I think. So what they said they would do was, if I could help them install some of their systems, they would try to organise a transfer for me to another InterContinental property somewhere as Assistant Front of House Manager and then I could build my career from there up. So I thought, "That sounds fair enough" and I think that's what they tried to do. But because, and I think people in chain companies will identify with this, I was never quite inside the company, I was always an outsider if you like.

A role came up at the Hôtel Le Grand in Paris, a big InterContinental property, and I didn't get that. I didn't really get a proper interview; I never got past someone in London to meet the General Manager. And the same thing happened with Chicago as well. You know that employment protection kicks in after two years and a week before my second anniversary at The Churchill, they called me in and said, "We're making you redundant. We haven't managed to find another post for you in the group. So that's it". That was a big shock – a betrayal actually – because I had done a lot on trust over six months bedding the new systems down.

As it turned out, I had been interviewing for a job with them for what was then The Britannia on Grosvenor Square, now The Millennium Mayfair. But because they wanted to make sure that they were inside the two years and thus I had no real employment rights, they didn't wait at The Churchill to see whether I was going to get offered that job – so I was effectively made redundant on the Friday and I happened to get a job offer from The Britannia on the following Monday. The job at The Britannia wasn't a job I particularly wanted, I have to say, because it was a lesser hotel in some respects though actually they were very similar hotels, with the same corporate accounts, only about 400 metres down the road. It was really awful to lose my job, awful – but it would have been far more damaging if I hadn't got the job offer on the Monday.

I worked at The Britannia for 20 months or so and I learnt all of the InterContinental's systems. As I look back now, I think that was a very good thing – I do know what the ratios for things should look like, more than if I had never worked outside of the independent sector, so a stint in one of these big chains is, I believe, a good thing.

I started at The Britannia and they didn't send me my redundancy cheque from The Churchill so I went to see the Personnel Manager at The Britannia and said, "I'm supposed to have got a settlement because I was made redundant at the last place". "Oh yeah, but because you got the job here straightaway, we take the view that you weren't redundant" and I said, "No, no. I have got a letter from you saying that I am going to get this amount of money because I'm being made redundant and that letter predates your offer by four days". "Well, you know, that's policy." So I rang up head office and asked John Wright if he would give me 10 minutes. To my surprise, he said, "Yes, come on in". So I went to see him and I explained what had happened.

John's reaction was "Take the job at The Britannia. I know you think it's a lesser job but you'll learn plenty. Take it – and on the money, ring up The Churchill and tell them you want the money. They can't have it both ways". So I rang The Churchill and said, "I think you ought to pay me this. I have been to see John Wright and he thinks you should pay me this". "Right then", and a cheque arrived a few days later. I'm not normally quite that angry or confrontational. I had started to question, "Is that the way it is then?" but then, in the meeting with John, I realised that no, that isn't the way it is and that's not the way he sought to run the organisation; it's just the way some more junior people have tried to interpret it. I realised that where I had the moral compass before was actually right and John confirmed that I was right and they were wrong – that was good.

So The Britannia was fine. I did quite well there, worked along, learnt a lot, worked with some great people that I'm still in touch with today. John Acton, the General Manager, and I never truly got on well but we developed a professional respect. He knew exactly what he was doing running that hotel – it ran very well, it ran very profitably, he really knew what he was doing – so I learnt a lot from him. Then the Front of House Manager post came up after about 18 months and I interviewed for it and I didn't get it. The guy that got it was nice enough – a fellow called Paul McMahon, who had been out in Bahrain for InterContinental. We actually got on well but as soon as that happened, I thought, "Right, I'm out of here. All these promises of work all around the world aren't coming off, a job's come up in a business that I know and I didn't get it, and I don't know if this firm is ever going to deliver for me".

Because I really wanted to leave, I looked at everything, things that I really shouldn't have been looking at as well things that I should. One job was for Front of House Manager here at Gleneagles. I had heard of the hotel, it had a good reputation. I had done a Fidelio installation at The Churchill; Gleneagles was on the cusp of a Fidelio installation about which they were quite worried. And I was prepared to move to Scotland too – I figured that if I was prepared to go to Chicago, what's the difference, Scotland's the same!

When I came for interview here, I had to come on a Sunday because I couldn't get any time off. I had met Peter Lederer in London and I was to interview with George Graham, who was the Operations Director here in those days. The hotel also used to have a retired Lt. Colonel, who was what did for guest relations in those days, a lovely gentleman called Ron Smith. He's since passed away, sadly. I turned up for interview here, having flown up and hired a car and got myself here. I remember getting about two miles out of the airport and thinking, "Blimey! There's not a lot here! This *is* countryside!". Ron greeted me in the lobby because as I walked in I was looking a bit lost and it was Sunday morning and very busy. I said, "I've got an appointment to see George Graham. Could you let him know I'm here, please?". He sat me down in what was then the Drawing Room and, bear in mind that if I got the job he would have been working for me and I was 26 at the time, he said, "May I inquire if you're here for the vacancy as Front of House Manager?". I said, "Of course, you may. Yes, I am". He shook my hand and said, "Very best of luck to you". I thought, "Goodness! I've come from London where it's dog-eat-dog. That was just fantastic". I had a more bruising interview with George, but he was trying to work whether I could do the job! I remember at the end of the interview – everything had gone well – George said, "If I can say it, you look very young" and I said, "Well, thank you, can I ask to say something to you? Can you not make that the reason you don't give me the job?". He burst out laughing and said, "OK, all right. You know you've got it". In fairness, he took a chance on me.

We worked together for quite some time. I had about four jobs here – they just sort of moved me around. First, I was Front of House Manager. Then they wanted to put this annualised hours system into food and beverage so they called me Operations Development Manager and I was looking after front of house as well as trying to organise this system for the 200-odd people we wanted to move onto these contracts, with a consultant. We got that done and then they more formally made me Operations Manager, so I looked after maintenance and few other bits and pieces, housekeeping and things like that.

I got married at the end of 1999 and that's when Patrick Elsmie joined the business. George went off to build Glenmor, our seasonal ownership business, to be our Development Director. They sat me down and said, "Right, we want to move some stuff on here. When the new GM starts, would you take a job that we want to call 'Head of Change'?". Everyone was saying, "Don't take it? It's like being put on projects. You'll be out of work in 12 months". And, of course, by that time I was 30, I'd been here four or five years and I was thinking, "Actually that mightn't be the worst thing in the world".

So I took the job and we did a wholesale re-organisation of sales, finance, and a whole host of things under this gentleman who was FD at the time. I learnt a vast amount. Sometimes it was quite difficult because it's almost like business process re-engineering where inevitably teams are going to get smaller not bigger as a consequence. But it was good experience, trying to do that humanely.

After a year or two, Patrick decided that he would have two hotel managers: one who looked after the front of house and one who looked after back of house. So for a year or two, I did the back of house bit, although I also looked after the front desk because I was experienced in that. Then after a year or two, Patrick decided he'd swap us around and that was great because then I was running the food and beverage department here and some other things of which I'd not really got a great deal of experience. When I looked down my CV, I found that at some point along the journey I had managed every single team at Gleneagles. So I knew the business inside out and everybody knew me, which is useful, for better or worse!

I did an MBA around the same time, a three-year part-time course at Strathclyde. I was 33 and Patrick asked, "Why do you want to be still sitting in seminars when you're 36 years old?". I said "I haven't been to university for 10 years now. This is where the future leaders are going to be. They're all going to have one of these". Everyone said, "Go for a week to Cranfield" but it's not the same in my view; you need exams, you need to meet people from different industries. The MBA taught me ever such a lot. We did statistical process control, quite advanced mathematics and quantitative methods that I hadn't done since I was in school, and I really found some of that quite tough – but I got through it. Then we got to marketing and HR and all these guys from British Aerospace and wherever were really struggling and I was thinking, "This is just common-sense". That was when the penny really dropped. I realised, "This why you do an MBA. So you truly understand what you're good at, where you are weaker" and that was fabulous, it really was. It was a game-changing experience for me, in terms of light-bulbs coming on and understanding. You think you're good at numbers because you can hold a P&L the right way up, but it doesn't make you good at numbers or analysis at all.

The MBA forced me a little bit. I thought, "I'm a bit stuck. I'm a hotel manager here. It's quite a good business but, because you've never been a general manager, you're probably going to have to go to a more modest business to be a general manager" and that was really difficult for me. I thought, "I don't want to go and run a 70-room hotel that is less good than this, just to be called GM."

And then an opportunity came along at Royal Bank of Scotland, which was developing its 125-acre campus at Gogarburn in Edinburgh. I interviewed with them and the fellow that was interviewing me said, "You just look too young for this job. Would you consider being the number two here, with a view to taking on the number one post on a fixed term contract, moving into it in 18 months?". I said, "Well, never say never. It's not what I came down here to talk to you about and, if you're just going to get some GM out of an average hotel in Edinburgh to run this and ask me to be his assistant, I'm not sure. But if you're going to hire the top person who runs EuroDisney or something like that and I'll be his number two, give me a ring". I heard nothing for four or five months and then one day, when I was in America with our sales rep in Connecticut, the phone rang, "I'd like to talk to you again about this RBS position". I said, "Well, that was a long time ago" and he said, "I know". The long and the short of it was that because Fred Goodwin was in charge of the bank, it had to be right and all the people they were talking to all said, "I want £200,000 or £250,000" and of course they were hoping to pay probably £60,000. I mean they had no idea what these sort of individuals cost and so bluntly, rather like The Churchill, I got back in the interview process because I was probably cheaper and less senior than these guys! So I interviewed with them again and we agreed terms. But even my terms, which were not generous at all, were too much for the bank (it's a bit like the Civil Service, they've got all these pay grades), so they said, "We work closely with Compass Group so we're going to get Compass Group to contract you and then Compass will just bill us for your salary and benefits – but you have to have an RBS pass and all of our staff have to think you work for RBS".

Anyway, I took the job and I'm really glad I did. It was an opening, full mobilisation: 3,200 office workers on the site, 250 service personnel, 15 different companies involved – Group 4, a cleaning company, Compass, hairdressers, Tesco, we had all sorts. So my role was to get all of that moving. It was quite difficult because culturally 15 different companies are not the same but you wanted to make the service brand, what they said to me was, "like Four Seasons". That was what they wanted, or like Gleneagles; they quite liked Gleneagles at RBS at that time.

That was probably the most stressful period of my working life because there was so little time. I joined them with three months or so to opening. The building wasn't finished, nobody was hired, and what you started to see about a month before opening was a retrenchment from people within the bank because there was a feeling that this was going to go wrong and so people were starting to put some distance between themselves and it in case it all hit the fan! So that was dead tough, but actually I learnt a lot about myself there – that's the calmest I have ever been at work. I look at myself now when I get a bit emotional and think, "What's wrong with you? This place runs like a song, it's fine".

I realised the service was going to be nowhere near what we really wanted because these people had had no training so I undertook to do a 30-minute 'here's what you do' toolbox talk for staff from the various service companies, such as Group 4 Securicor, about what service means. Many of these guys only had 15 seconds with a customer, so if you do three or four things right in that time, that's going to be a start – and so it transpired. I was talking to 55-year-old men working for Group 4, "Make sure you look at people. Make sure you speak first – always, always you. Why? Because it's good" and they did it. "Good morning." In all the other RBS businesses, the security guard didn't say "Good morning", he just checked your pass. So the bank loved it, and the staff were getting all these plaudits for the service, which in turn were reinforcing and developing the behaviour. I took a lot out of that because you don't know what makes you different until you go to a different environment like that and then you find out.

We got Gogarburn open, to a great sense of relief. So we then had a real honeymoon period after it was open, culminating in an official opening by HM The Queen. We then opened the business school, which was the second wave of the campus, with lecture theatres modelled on Harvard and 68 bedrooms, and we bedded the service down properly. Then my boss within Compass, who ran the whole RBS account, decided to move on and, basically, he gave me his job – he said, "You'll do this". RBS weren't totally delighted about me not being at Gogarburn all the time but thankfully we made them see that they could have the same service standard across their 60 sites across the UK and Ireland if they let me do this job because I could replicate that standard nationally. And so we did for a couple of years – we had 18 or 19 clusters across the country, each with what we called a front of house service manager, and we were providing a range of services to 60,000 or 70,000 of their people with a team of 1,200 people. Sadly, much of it has been undone since the whole banking world fell apart. But then midway through that last year, Patrick Elsmie from here was going to become the Managing Director, so he called me up and said, "Would you come back to Gleneagles as General Manager?".

When I got that call from Patrick, it was an interesting time because we were rebidding the RBS contract and it was quite a bruising process. In those days, aside from the GPO contract, it was the biggest national business and industry contract that Compass had in the UK. We were looking for a five-year deal so we were bidding on about £300m worth all told – and the bank had introduced some new people into purchasing who were just difficult, deliberately difficult I thought. So when Patrick called, I really wrestled with it. I thought, "GM of Gleneagles, it's a great job, it really is. If someone had said when I was in college that, at 37 or 38, I would be GM at Gleneagles, I'd have said, 'I'll take that, thank you very much'. But here, I've got all this autonomy, my bosses leave me alone because we're doing the business for RBS. I don't know if I can go back to going to the same place to work every day. But on the other side I have a baby daughter, and I've been away a lot as the first one grew up". In the end I persuaded myself, "If Real Madrid are the best football team and you've played for them once, if you get the chance to play for them again and they're still the best football team, what should you do? Play for the second best football team?". So that was the view I took with Gleneagles: it is probably one of the best hotel jobs in the UK, if not the best hotel job, owned and managed by the same company with a great deal of autonomy. So I chose to come back.

The timing was most fortunate because I came back right at the death of 2007 and in 2008 of course the world fell over and the client entertaining side of RBS was just decimated. It wasn't easy here either, I have to say, our business dipped too but it's a much more supportive environment, your team is much more local here, you see them everyday. Having got used to travelling almost all the time with RBS, I found it really difficult the first two or three months, just coming in here every morning. I was bidding with Patrick to work from home a day or two a week but he wasn't a fan of that at all because he's a very traditional hotelier, "How can you be a hotelier working from home? You're supposed to be meeting guests" and, of course, he was right!

As the years have gone on since then, it's become more natural and that's been really great. Patrick was busily handing things over from the start of 2013, quite conscious that he was retiring so I have had the run of the place, with him, for the last two years. Certainly I have had a lot of autonomy. Diageo is a very hands-off owner – we have a call once a month and we meet them maybe once or twice a year. As long as we're doing what we said we were going to do – making the planned amount of money, winning some awards, making them look good generally, not getting in the newspapers for all the wrong reasons!

I came back as General Manager and became MD last year. The Ryder Cup was a big distraction last year, there was a lot going on with that. The Ryder Cup is a funny thing – people on the outside of it think that Gleneagles had to organise all of it, and people on TV use all this hyperbole "the biggest TV audience in the world". But actually the reality is that you're on a team of multi-agencies, with lots of people involved, and that in itself is hugely educative. Very often, we'd go to a meeting where there might have been 18 people from various public sector bodies around the table and a couple of people from Ryder Cup Europe and a couple of people from Gleneagles – it's a very big machine indeed. But ultimately you are the venue and you are trying to make sure that nothing anybody else does is going to adversely impact your reputation and also your on-going operability, looking after guests. Everybody says, "You must have really focused on the Ryder Cup". Ironically, last year, the big message here was "Let's make sure that we never get a guest letter this year that says, 'I didn't have such a good stay because you were all distracted with the Ryder Cup'. Let's make sure we don't get one of those before the Ryder Cup or after it". If you came to stay here three weeks before the Ryder Cup, I think you still had a fantastic time and if you came three days afterwards, you still had a fantastic time. In some ways, I'm more proud of the team for achieving that than having delivered on the event. You're always going to deliver on the event because, in some ways, it was similar when I opened Gogarburn. What I learnt from Gogarburn and the Ryder Cup was the same: some of these things actually do get too big to fail because there are so many other people with so much to lose if it goes wrong as well – between you, you just make sure it doesn't go wrong!

That said, the Ryder Cup was a great occasion. It was great to have the teams here. The television exposure was quite phenomenal and we were blessed with weather – we were so fortunate in comparison to our colleagues in Ireland and Wales, though they may have enjoyed better golf!

I think the Ryder Cup demonstrated a level of capability here. We learnt a lot about ourselves there and I think we have, as a result of it, a really great team.

Paul Heery and I are just finding our way at the moment because we have only just worked with each other for the past couple of months but yesterday afternoon our HR Director said to me, "Paul had all of the key function heads in this afternoon for a meeting. He wanted to make sure that they all understood that we had potential investors in from Monday next week so he's got everybody to make sure the grass is cut properly, everything's painted". I had put that at the bottom of my To Do list for this morning and I just thought, "Wow, what a weight off! It's Wednesday afternoon and he's just done it!". That's largely why he's here but it's great. I don't have to ask him, he's already thinking, "What's the business going to need next week? Let's get that done". That's what the beauty of the team here is: I won't say you have people to catch you when you fall, you've got people who make sure you never do. We all end up looking good but actually it's a product of a lot of people thinking about what's the right thing to do here. It's a great company, with great people. I don't think it's the same in every business but I do think good hotels are a little bit like, I don't like the term 'family' but they're just a great place, so many like-minded people who genuinely care, I suppose.

When I came here the first time, in 1995, I called up John Wright and said, "Thank you for whatever you must have said" since I assumed Gleneagles had taken a reference from him and he said, "No, they didn't call me". So I went to see George Graham, my boss, and said, "I'm sure you took references on me. Somebody must have said the right thing because I'm here. Could you tell me who you called so I can thank them?" and he said, "No. I won't tell you. But yes, I talked to some people and I got told you're a workaholic and that I should take you on". I said, "OK, fine, but could you tell me who it was?" and he said, "No", so to this day I don't know who gave me that reference! And exactly the same thing happened when I went to RBS: when I thanked Patrick, he said, "They didn't call me". So I share this thought with young people whenever I speak to them: most of my jobs have been an old boss ringing me up and asking me to come and work for him, and in the other ones somebody has taken me on but they haven't asked my boss for a reference, because they'd asked somebody else who I must have come into contact with, maybe I worked alongside, maybe knew of me. So what I always tell people is "Never burn a relationship. Never treat anybody badly". What goes around does come around, the world is very small.

I also say to young people "Never stop learning". I gave a speech to some graduating students a couple of years ago and urged them to think of themselves as being an iPhone – because everybody wants one, it's appealing, it's good looking and it does many things well. The world of employment is no different: turn up, look smart, look like you can do something useful and that you're not going to make it difficult for somebody.

The other thing that I have learnt – and I still don't do enough of it – is that most managers spend most of their time worrying about or dealing with the bottom 10% of their performers. In actual fact, we'd probably get far further if we invested that time in the top 20% telling them what a great job they're doing and showing them how they could do it even

better – it would be like letting the genie out of the bottle. Another thing is that if you look at really great chief executives, of big businesses, they never make anything sound complicated. Everything sounds really simple, because they have thought it all through and they don't feel the need to impress people with all the mindless business babble. They just say, "Here's what we need to do" and I'm a big admirer of that.

I think that some general managers are really unfortunate because you have to work so hard to get that position and you're not a hotelier when you get there. It should be a great job, it should be the prize, but instead sadly the reality for many people in that position is that all you end up doing is answering loads of questions an asset manager asks you. What the owner really wants you to do is to tell him how the business can be better or make more money but it's as if the industry is letting the view that they're not good enough to do that become the reality because they're not pushing back against it.

When I worked at The Britannia, John Acton had plans to redevelop an internal car park space into a ballroom, because the hotel didn't have a ballroom. It was a fantastic idea, just what that hotel should have done, but no one did it. Actually that was his job, to say, "Look, I'm running at 91% occupancy at the moment. That's my rate. Frankly, there's no upside on this business, but I've had a look and I think we can create a big upside by adding a big ballroom". That's asset management, actually, and it used to be encouraged. I think perhaps owners would get more out of their assets if they asked the GM on the ground, "What's the pinchpoint? What's holding us up here?" instead of getting analysts and asset managers to do it.

Certainly, we're lucky enough to have that approach here. There's a whole shopping list of things we have shown Diageo. We're doing a couple of them and we're not doing some others and that's absolutely fine. I'm one of the lucky people because I have got an owner that looks at me as managing an asset interest as well as managing the business but I'm aware that over the last 20 years that's less the norm.

Too often, GMs are just a sort of operations manager. And if that's the job, well at Premier Inn, which I think is a great hotel company, among the best, at 26 years old you could be running a dozen hotels! Good for you, great! You'll be well paid, it's a good job, and if that's what you want to do, that's great. It's not what I chose to do. When people ask, I say, "Do you want to do it in five star as GM? It's a long haul, you'll have to manage just about every department on your way up. You certainly will if you're in the Four Seasons or Mandarin Oriental or any of those groups. And then you've got to wait for a position to come available – you have to be patient. If you're very impatient to be called 'manager' and have a company car, well you'll get there a lot quicker in a Premier Inn!".

The key to being a great hotelier is emotional intelligence. I float around and most of the guests know who I am. They're not particularly bothered about talking to me but they like the fact that I'm taking the trouble – as Paul does – of walking around and taking the pulse of the place to know what going on here. At induction, I always talk about the grotty English phrase, "Treat everybody the way you want to be treated". That's rubbish: treat people the way *they* want to be treated. The analogy I give is that, to talk to a four-year-old, adults bend down, get down to their level but we don't make the same adjustment for an adult. If somebody's obviously in a hurry, he's in a bloody hurry, meet him halfway! If someone wants to chat, chat to them. And that's what we encourage our people to do. I don't think you're teaching emotional intelligence. I think you're just saying to people, "Give some thought to the fact that you're not actually there to just stick a registration card in front of them and ask them to sign it". Once you couch it like that, you tell waiters, "You're not serving food. You're creating a two-hour experience for people in celebration of their 40th birthday. The fact they're going to eat a meal during that period is largely incidental". I think a lot of the team are quite surprised by that but I really believe that if you're going to get people to do what you need them to do, truly to deliver service, they've just got to do it as naturally as they possibly can and think about, just think about, the person. It's consideration, isn't it really, emotional intelligence?

The numbers aren't unimportant in five star hotels but I believe that, if we get the service right, if we really look after the customers, if we make sure we give them what they want not what we want to do, I won't say that the numbers will take care of themselves but they are an outcome. We don't start with "We've got to get to that number" because if you do, that's when you start making stupid cost-based decisions. Danny Meyer, the New York restaurateur, said this wonderfully, "When I'm a customer, I'm asking myself a question of the service, 'Are you doing something *for* me or are you doing something *to* me?'". Michael Heppell has another way of putting it, "How would you serve that person if they were famous? If it was David Beckham sitting at the table, would your service be any different to the service you're about to give the person who's actually there?".

What makes a world class hotel? People make it happen, the collective will to be the best. It was an off-the-cuff remark I made at one of our management meetings a few years ago when we were discussing our Leading Quality score and we'd got the second rank scoring – there are only three or four hotels in Scotland in it. I said, "Let's get behind this. We're better than that score and I didn't come here to work at the second best hotel in Scotland. I'm going to book another one of these inspections". And it was one of our managers, for one of the pursuits outside, who said afterwards, "That was really great. None of us want to work at the second best hotel in Scotland either".

The other thing that's been helpful here is that we don't have a regime change every two years. We have a lot of stability of leadership and also stability within some of the teams. Hoteliers elsewhere would give their eye-teeth for that stability! The accumulated knowledge, the relationships, people not scoring points off one another, people assuming good intent on both sides, people not trying to arm-wrestle each other to the floor to get a promotion. In my view, the biggest obstacle to speed of execution in business generally between organisations and within organisations is trust – lawyers make millions out of it, or the lack of it! And the sort of stability we have here builds that trust.

You build trust by how you act, the way in which you conduct yourself. When we get into potentially difficult or adversarial situations, quite a disarming thing is to say, "What's the right thing to do here?" or "What's fair?". I use that with guests quite a lot, if things have gone wrong, "What's the fair thing to do here?". Most people react really well to that.

It's said that the customer is always right. But, like any hotel, we do have horrendous examples of where people were being actually quite unreasonable. But when they say things on Twitter or Facebook, it's because they are angry with the company – they're not really angry with a meal, rather they feel something's gone wrong, the trust's been breached, the brand hasn't done what it said it was going to do. And if you frame it in that way, you can sit down with people in difficult situations and reach a sensible solution.

We have an interesting situation here – most of our business, more than 80%, comes to us directly. We use only one OTA, booking.com. Doing the sums, I think we probably are saving money by running a reservations team of about 12 people, which is colossal for the number of rooms we've got. It's a big bill, but I still think it's cheaper than the alternative – and our TREVPAR is through the roof! Our team is trying to sell dinner, horse-riding and a round of golf as well as a room. So it works for our business – and it happened that way largely because we're hopeless with technology and we didn't get that far on the web; it's not because we're strategically excellent, by the way! But I look back on it now and I think, "But for the grace of God, we could have driven all our customers online" and effectively lost them.

To someone already in the business aspiring to get to the very top, I'd say, "Don't look for shortcuts. You've just got to make more impact than the next guy". If you really want to get to the top, there's a lot of hotels and in our industry, certainly at unit level, if I can call it that rather unattractive term, endeavour is more often than not a match for academia. Hard work works. It takes a long time sometimes to understand that.

If things aren't going right, don't be afraid to move, you've got to be willing to change. I talk to youngsters about how I really admire the way some popstars re-invent themselves; they get themselves to a point of success and then throw it all away; they discard it and they start again.

There's a big thing in America that they call 'CX', an abbreviation for customer experience, and that's what I was doing in RBS. I believe we will continue to see this sector seeking to attract people out of the hotel business to deliver the service in these offices so that the very highly-paid people who drive investment banks and law firms actually get a great experience. Goldman Sachs and Clifford Chance, for example, have been doing this well and you are seeing it now elsewhere – that's an opportunity for hoteliers that perhaps have had enough of hotels.

To someone thinking of going into the hotel business, I'd urge them to think through what it's going to look like when they're at a different age and stage of life – for example, if they have a family what's it going to look like. I think hoteling can be a lot of fun, you work with some nice people, it's a job that going to be around so it's quite a good bet in that regard – customer experience, customer service, the consumer culture isn't going to go away. But make sure that you get into a bit of it where the people part is going to continue to be a part of what the customers want rather than a part that might just get taken out by technology.

GREG LIDDELL

Mandarin Oriental Hotel, Barcelona

Park Hyatt, Sydney

Le Meridien, Sydney

Āman Resorts

Karma Resorts

Mandarin Oriental Dhara Dhevi, Chiang Mai

Landmark Mandarin Oriental, Hong Kong

Mandarin Oriental, Barcelona

Question always what you are doing and why.
Don't turn on the blinkers and become robotic.

I was born in Mexico City. My mother is Mexican; my father is Australian – many would consider this an unusual mix. My father worked for Qantas Airways and was posted outside of Australia for many years of his career with the airline, which led him to meeting my mother in Mexico City during the time he was stationed there. I am the youngest of four brothers, all of us being born in Mexico City. The reality, however, is that we have spent little time physically living in Mexico. Mexico City was a base for my parents during their time living in various countries across the globe. I was fortunate enough to live in Tahiti, French Polynesia and subsequently Rome through the work postings of my father, although I returned to Sydney, Australia, at a relatively young age and was educated there.

My mother was also in the travel business, which further facilitated traveling for the family. Once we returned to live in Sydney, we had the good fortune to see some fantastic destinations across the globe and, of course, with that came the exposure to hotels and resorts.

Having lived in various countries, I believe this provided me with the facility to learn languages. I definitely consider this a gift handed to me. It certainly beats learning a language in a classroom … Interestingly enough, growing up and being educated in Sydney, at that time it wasn't particularly common to speak or focus on additional languages; part of that stems from the sheer distance of Australia from the likes of Europe, despite being a largely multicultural society. Apart from an early passion or interest in hotels, I would comfortably say that the exposure of travelling to various parts of the world and speaking languages other than English were strong influencers that likely led me to the world of hospitality and hotels and resorts.

Looking at the ancestral roots of my family, the backgrounds of my father and mother differed and contrasted and this also likely influenced in me an ability to adapt to cultures and customs with little effort.

I continue to have a significant attachment to Australia. In addition to being close to my family, I retain close contact with a large group of friends whom I grew up with – they're still a great group of 'mates', as we would say in Australia! I value that – they're very down-to-earth, fantastic people.

When did I realise that I wanted to work in this particular environment? I don't recall any one particular instance, to be honest. I always had a great interest in the world of travel and particularly hotels; perhaps if it wasn't going to be hotels, I may have opted for airlines. Certainly a contributing factor was the strong desire I had from an early age to please people and the satisfaction I gained from doing so. The attraction of seeing new destinations and experiencing cultures always existed and the hotel environment was an obvious vehicle to take me on this path. The vastly different cultures and walks of life one sees in a hotel were always intriguing to me and, finally, meeting people and interacting with people was always something that came easily to me – it's something I continue to enjoy.

I came to know of Āman Resorts perhaps six months after it was founded (the first Āman resort being Āmanpuri in Phuket, Thailand, opened by my great friend Anthony Lark, who now operates the well-known Trisara Resort in Phuket today). The impact made on me was immediate. The resorts were certainly ahead of their time when they were developed in the late 1980s and early 1990s by Adrian Zecha.

The first Āman experience I had was at Āmankila in Bali. The impact of the setting and the service culture was significant and stayed with me as I reaffirmed in my mind that this was the type of environment I wanted to develop a career in. An outstanding service experience was created by Adrian Zecha that went beyond nice bathroom amenities, champagne on ice and high thread counts of bed linen.

In the case of Āmankila, the resort architecture was designed by the remarkable Ed Tuttle. Here's the point of difference: Ed Tuttle creates the bones of the resort with Adrian Zecha; following his design, he then has absolute influence on many soft aspects of the resort – for example, the colour of the bougainvillea planted by a terrace, how a table will be set and what kind of show plate will be presented for breakfast. The detail and yet the simplistic nature of what was being delivered was, and is, outstanding. Ed Tuttle, working with Adrian Zecha, the founder of Āman Resorts, is an incredible combination.

When Āman Resorts came into being in 1998, it was considered absurd to think that a resort of only 40 suites or pavilions, opened on an expansive piece of property with a staff to guest ratio of three to one, charging US$500 per night might stand a chance, let alone be successful. Today, I am confident Adrian Zecha looks back with a smile.

Prior to Āman Resorts, Adrian Zecha was involved and in fact was the co-founder of Regent Hotels & Resorts. Originally an accomplished journalist, half-Indonesian, half-Dutch, he spent many years in Hong Kong. He found himself in the hotel business with the famous Bob Burns and Georg Rafael and together they founded Regent Hotels & Resorts. The Regent of

Hong Kong opened in 1980, later became The Inter-Continental Hotel and was recently sold by the group itself for the significant sum of $938 million. The collection included the well-known Regent of Sydney (now a Four Seasons Hotel many years later), and the iconic Beverly Wilshire Hotel, also now a Four Seasons Hotel. Adrian Zecha, Bob Burns and Georg Rafael to a great extent set the tone for 'luxury hotel chains', particularly in the US and Australasia in the 1970s and early 1980s.

Following the sale of Regent International Hotels, most of which became Four Seasons Hotels or Resorts, these three individuals went off to develop their own hotels and / or resorts. As mentioned, Adrian Zecha of course went on to create Āman Resorts in 1988. Georg Rafael created the famous and highly-regarded Rafael Hotel Group, which he subsequently sold to Mandarin Oriental Hotel Group in 2000, and finally Bob Burns, amongst other properties, created Villa Feltrinelli in Gargano, Italy. I talk about these individuals simply because of my admiration for them and the influence they have had on my career path, particularly as I look back.

When I completed secondary school, I studied a commerce degree at university but chose to do this on a part-time basis so I could work full-time in a hotel and start my career at an early age. I joined The Park Hyatt in Sydney, a well-known, outstanding property, and certainly at the time and most likely up until now, Sydney's premier hotel. I started as a bellman and worked my way through various departments of the hotel. By the time I finished with my studies, I had made my way to a mid-level manager's position. In hindsight, having started to work in the industry at an early age allowed me the opportunity take on a General Manager position at age 27 with the prestigious Āman Resort group.

I recall my time at The Park Hyatt with very fond memories. There was a great camaraderie, particularly amongst the chaps working as bell attendants in the early days. We had a great sense of pride in what we did; we worked as a team to complete what needed to be done; however, just as importantly, we had one hell of a good time doing it and there wasn't a guest who did not feel that. An element of this experience stays with me today and is something I consistently try to promote in any hotel or resort I find myself in.

I later joined Le Meridien Hotel Sydney, one of a number of hotels that opened in Sydney prior to Sydney hosting the Olympic Games in 2000. There was an undersupply of hotels at the time and a number of five star properties opened their doors during that period. Le Meridien was a much larger hotel in terms of inventory, with 415 rooms and suites, and the exposure to a larger hotel was important for me in terms of rounding my experience. The pre-opening experience was exceptional and rewarding and countless anecdotes exist until today about the race to the finish line in opening the hotel on time. Escorting guests on particular routes to their rooms in order to avoid wet paint was no small feat at the time, given most walls of the guest corridors and spaces had been finished minutes before the guests arrived!

After three years at Le Meridien, Sydney, I was asked to join the Raffles Hotel, Sydney (Merchant Court), which had recently opened. This was an unintended and very brief stop in my journey; I believe I was there for no longer than 10 months before having the opportunity to interview with Āman Resorts in Indonesia.

This was my first step in taking my journey overseas. The interview process was extensive and included a visit to head office in Singapore to meet with the then Chairman, Adrian Zecha. Impossible not to be impressed by him, the question was how I was going to impress him. I then went on to visit the intended property in Bali and meet with the Regional Head of Āman Resorts Bali, Guy Heywood, who remains a great friend of mine.

I often recount the story of Guy interviewing me in his home in Bali. Following a brief introduction, he asked me to head to his music system and change the music to my liking. I was suspicious and rightly so. He was keen to know what music I would select and how I would adapt to the situation. I selected a Cuban CD by The Buena Vista Social Club, which not only led to a conversation about Spanish-speaking countries, it also led to continuing our conversation with two very large cigars in hand. Needless to say, the meeting went well. Guy Heywood's strategy to create a 'situation' and monitor my reaction has stuck with me. Guy may well have forgotten about this episode – or perhaps not, I have never discussed it with him. His strategy makes great sense: we serve our guests daily; each and every guest is unique and different and this calls on us to adapt in all senses of the word. Simple, but brilliant.

The vast array of personalities and backgrounds that we are required to interact with is quite astounding – this is what I remain passionate about. We create and facilitate individual experiences that encapsulate comfort, convenience and, most importantly, guest recognition. Often easier said than done! There have been so many instances wherein I have witnessed brilliance from managers, colleagues and guests for that matter and equally instances where I perhaps wished I was not present – however, these latter experiences have provided tremendous opportunities to grow and learn. Plagiarism in the right sense can be very useful.

In the hospitality business, and particularly in luxury businesses or brands that charge what many consider to be a great deal of money, focusing on and paying attention to detail is critical. The success of a hotel or resort is regularly measured by the infinite attention we give to the most minor aspects that define a great hotel. Perfection is what we strive for, certainly difficult if not impossible to attain at times and equally we all have instances where something goes horribly wrong, leaving us bewildered and scratching our heads. Thankfully these instances of horror are few and far between. A negative experience often seems far worse to a hotel colleague than it might to the guest. The strength of a team comes when an issue is dealt with rapidly and to the fullest extent possible. If we have dropped the ball, have we been able pick the ball up off the floor and run with it?

"No detail is too small": this is often a message we wave across our back-of-house corridors in the pursuit of great things. We do, however, often run the risk of creating robots in our teams as we strive for perfection and follow the suggested guidelines and procedures. It is for this reason that a great General Manager is a fixture in the lobby or breakfast dining room of a hotel or resort, leading from the front and helping the team to adjust to guests and their specific needs, helping to produce the 'theatre' of the day. First impressions are lasting ones, this is so true of our industry – for example, a great initial interaction at the reservation stage and a great arrival experience will, in nearly all cases, lead to a happy guest departure. In fact, I would argue you almost need to try to 'spoil' the guest experience if guests leave disheartened following a great arrival.

I originally interviewed with Āman Resorts for a position in Bali at the Āmandari Resort Ubud. I never got to Āmandari – the destination changed and I was scheduled instead to go to the Āmanpuri Resort in Phuket to run the villa operations of this stunning property. With this, I left Australia and headed towards Phuket. Eventually, following my orientation with Āman Resorts, I found myself in the Philippines as manager of the incredible Āmanpulo Resort, a private island with its own aviation operation and airstrip. Nothing else exists on the island: it's a completely self-contained 97-hectare island, self-sufficient in terms of energy, water supply, aviation, beautiful guest accommodations or pavilions and a superb villa operation. Hands down the whitest sand in the world, complemented by an incredibly talented staff of Filipinos.

Following Āmanpulo Resort, I spent time with Āman Resorts in the USA and Mexico. Throughout my time with Āman Resorts in Indonesia, Thailand, Philippines and the USA, I developed some great friendships with colleagues and guests, many of which continue until today. It is a very small industry we work and live in; as the world becomes smaller, we often find ourselves looking after many common repeat guests or working with colleagues in new environments.

I joined Karma Resorts in 2004 and was employed by the very charismatic entrepreneur and Chairman of the company, John Spence. John, an unashamed 'Āmanjunkie' (a regular visitor to many Āman Resorts), had the idea of developing his own resorts with the premise that his concept would cater to families and a younger demographic. John purchases large plots of land and funds the subsequent development of the resort by selling varying types of beautifully appointed private luxury villas to individuals who seek a second home or are simply attracted by the investment, attaching the resort amenities to the development, which include spas, restaurants, beach clubs, kids clubs etc, thus creating an Āman-esque experience. His resorts are branded as Karma Resorts and affiliated with Leading Hotels of the World.

We opened the first Karma Resort property in Bali. A second property soon followed in Koh Samui, Thailand, followed by a stunning third property in Bali, called Karma Kandara, on the southernmost tip of the island. Karma also opened in Greece and the South of France. By the time I reached almost six years with John, we had accomplished a great deal and had many fantastic experiences. We equally went through challenging periods, which included the horrendous and heinous bombing blasts on the very peaceful island of Bali. Gentle and very spiritual people who respect all cultures were targeted purely because their island catered to Western tourists, namely Australians in this case.

Karma was about creating a new group of resorts, which required entrepreneurial flair on the part of John and a team around him that was able to very quickly adapt, execute and deliver. A remarkable experience all around. John Spence remains a respected and great friend today. I thoroughly enjoyed working between the Thai and Balinese or Javanese cultures throughout my tenure with Karma Resorts. Although perhaps wary at first, in addition to being very warm cultures, the colleagues in all of the locations quickly became an extension of the 'family'.

Is there a difference between running a luxury resort and running a city centre five star hotel? Fundamentally any hotel or resort operation operates under the premise of serving guests to the best of our ability, delivering the basics – a very comfortable bed, great water pressure in the bathroom, absolute cleanliness and a sumptuous breakfast. Getting these basic elements right is not negotiable; the stand-out hotels and resorts are those that aim to exceed expectations of guests at every turn.

A leisure guest will likely be spending valuable free time (a precious thing these days) to rest, recuperate, sight-see and enjoy. Business travellers are more often than not seeking comfort, intuitive service and convenience. Certainly resorts in terms of a maintenance scope are often more complex and involved, given the sheer foot-print of the property which is, by standard, larger. Barcelona is for all intents and purposes considered a city and yet the guests we welcome each day are predominately here for leisure purposes. The average length of stay of a guest in Barcelona is longer than in many city destinations as there is so much to do and see. It is our responsibility to ensure that our guests are steered in the right direction and make best use of their time with us. The opportunity to build a rapport and a relationship with guests in both city and resort destinations exists, in fact it exists in every hotel in the world. A corporate guest, for example, although limited in time, is likely to come back more than once to the hotel as a repeat client, so recognising a guest never goes unappreciated.

As far as operating a city hotel or resort is concerned, the objectives of running the hotel, therefore the room component, the business of restaurants, spas, retail space, transportation services, etc and the reporting that comes with managing the business is largely the same. Coupled with Finance and Sales & Marketing activity, it is often said that a General Manager of a hotel or resort is a 'jack of all trades and master of none'; given the number of business units that can exist within a hotel, the saying is not too farfetched.

I departed Karma Resorts to join Mandarin Oriental Hotel Group. I'm presently in my seventh year now with Mandarin Oriental Hotel Group. I started with the group in Chiang Mai, in the north of Thailand, at the magical Mandarin Oriental Dhara Dhevi. It was an outstanding resort and Victoria and I were pleased to be there for exactly three years. The resort was built on 65 acres and only five years old when we arrived. It had been built to reflect a Lana kingdom that existed 150 years ago. Over 2,000 trees were planted throughout the property, 400 of which were more than 100 years old and brought from the north of Thailand and Laos. The architecture and the materials used throughout were unique to put it mildly, which made for a significant burden on our maintenance team but certainly one that was heavily appreciated and valued by guests. The team that formed part of Dhara Dhevi were rich in culture and very warm and kind. The elegance of the Northern Thai people, and all Thai people, is indeed very special.

Following three years with Mandarin Oriental Dhara Dhevi, Chiang Mai, I was offered the opportunity to move to Hong Kong, to the Landmark Mandarin Oriental. There are two Mandarin Oriental Hotel properties in Hong Kong, one being the iconic flagship of the Group which opened its doors in 1963 in the heart of Central and the other which sits almost next door, being the modern and very chic Landmark Mandarin Oriental. The Mandarin Oriental Hong Kong closed for a brief period in 2006 to undergo a full refurbishment during which time The Landmark Mandarin Oriental, Hong Kong, opened its doors.

After many years of being focused on resorts, I had returned to a city environment. A significant change of scenery. Hong Kong is an outstanding city, as is the hotel I was privileged to manage. I think if you are presented the opportunity to work in any city, Hong Kong is surely up there with the best of them. It's a buzzing and vibrant environment that is open for business seven days a week. Hong Kong literally does not sleep. Both Mandarin Oriental Hotels in Hong Kong have the good fortune to be a regular meeting point, a dining destination or getaway to the respective spas for the locals of Hong Kong. With this, both hotels have a great sense of place, with a great connection to the local community. The work ethic and the efficiency, which somehow managed to be very warm, always amazed me about the great team of colleagues at The Landmark Mandarin Oriental.

I soon found myself after almost three years in Hong Kong headed to Mandarin Oriental, Barcelona. The opportunity to work in Europe for the first time was appealing, as was the great attraction of the hotel and the incredible city that is Barcelona, which is now home for Victoria and me. Following almost 10 months in the city, whilst feeling we could have easily spent more time in Hong Kong, Barcelona has become home very quickly.

One always hopes that the various steps taken in a career lead to progression and positive outcomes. Mandarin Oriental Hotel Group is an outstanding group to work with, having 30 hotels and resorts in operation and a great pipeline of future developments. A unique attribute of Mandarin Oriental Hotel Group is its active partnership and participation in both management and equity shareholding of a number of the Group's hotels. This sends a great message to potential investors that Mandarin Oriental knows its business and has 'skin in the game'. The focus is very much placed on being a luxury brand focused on quality and being best in class. It is certainly nice to surround yourself in an environment where the collective objective of the group and the chief executive is to consistently aim to deliver exactly that.

Over time, I have had fantastic experiences that include not only meeting celebrities, dignitaries and royalty; I have also met an abundance of exceptional human beings from all walks of life and varied backgrounds and as outlined earlier many relationships developed dating back a number of years still very much exist today. The interactions and protocols associated with heads of state and royalty are always interesting to be part of and the point I would make is that we often neglect to remember that, despite the circumstance and the respect and courtesy that one is required to extend, they do like to be as 'normal' as possible.

An Australian Prime Minister is a good example. He had been very recently elected to the Prime Ministership prior to attending a Global Warming Conference with key members of his cabinet. They had limited preparation time for the trade and diplomacy ahead of them, so shortly after their arrival to the resort, the Prime Minister of Australia was borrowing a shirt from me ... this only after I suggested that a suit and tie in Bali may not be the best option.

The business we are in allows us to have access to people we perhaps otherwise would not normally interact with. I have often noted that I find guests on holidays in particular are more open and willing to engage with 'strangers' who happen to be hotel management or colleagues ... and with that forms some excellent relationships that we value greatly.

In an effort to avoid robotic and stiff environments for guests, I comfortably tell teams I work with that, for as long as we are never over-familiar, we should be willing to engage with guests and go beyond the standards set in relation to our interaction with guests. Intuitively, we should also be able to read when a guest wishes to be left alone.

With English being a second language in the majority of countries that I have worked in, mistakes in the first instance generally occur as a result of making assumptions, which comes from the lack of confidence to check facts with guests. With the 'risk' of checking for understanding with guests and our desire to avoid inconveniencing a guest for a brief moment, we are often witness to monumental errors.

The industry sees itself as being innovative, often at the cost of dehumanising the experience for guests. Adam Tihany, the well-known designer based in New York and at the forefront of restaurant design, has often said that we should not try to emulate the 'home away from home' experience for our guests; in fact, he suggests we should forget home and provide something exciting and different in terms of design. Certainly this is a shift from the traditional tag line of hotels and resorts that claim to provide a home-like experience.

The food and beverage scene within hotels is evolving rapidly. In Asia, it has long been common to seek a great dining experience in a hotel or resort. If you live in Hong Kong, many of the best restaurants are located in hotels. This is definitely not true of Sydney, for example; however, we see this changing and a great example is the Mandarin Oriental, London, on Hyde Park, which is home to Dinner by Heston Blumenthal and Daniel Boulud's restaurant, Bar Boulud. Certainly I think the gastronomic experience in hotels will only develop and become more and more important with many of the globe's culinary experts taking on celebrity status and a 'cult'-like following of food *aficionados* growing rapidly. It's critical, however, to get the basics such as breakfast, in-room dining and a comfort food menu right before venturing out to more elaborate or distinct offerings.

The same can be said of spas. The Mandarin Oriental in Bangkok was, for its kind, the first hotel to have a spa. That concept blossomed and spread all over the world and spas became the norm – today it's perhaps viewed as strange that a hotel wouldn't have a spa. And the world of spas is evolving: many consumers use the term 'wellness' as opposed to 'spa' – with that comes nutrition, a sense of wellbeing, guided meditation and the list continues. Preventative medical based, non-invasive treatments are certainly the trend.

There is disruption in the industry now, which is mainly caused by technology. Airbnb, for example, is in some cases competing with hotels and resorts; the same leisure traveller is able to secure access to a private apartment or home complete with housekeeping services, a full fridge or 'mini bar' and access to maintenance if required, all through the simple navigation of a website. With a number of positives comes the downside of technology causing the interaction with guests to be far more limited – for example, automatic dialling and keypads to order room service, log wake up calls, etc. This is a risk the industry runs, particularly in the luxury high-end segment. Having said that, guests will always seek a seamless experience.

Other trends? Our ability to stretch beyond the norm, provide activities and experiences that guests are not able to normally take advantage of at home. Exclusive access to gourmet experiences, elite medical practitioners, world-famous attractions, bespoke and uniquely tailored experiences will always win the day for guests.

Moving forward, the market to which we sell suites will continue to grow; an emphasis will be placed on time spent away from home that is focused on the luxury of space and downtime. Many of our guests live in a very 'busy' world.

Personality plays – and will continue to play – a big part in the success of one's role in the hospitality world. Humility is a good thing. It's important to manage upwards and downwards and equally it's important to manage other people's personalities too. It's people who can quite easily make or break an experience. The product or the hardware can be wonderful; however, if that is not supported and complemented by the right people, who want to be in their roles, the experience does not form well at all.

I go out of my way to set my expectations of colleagues in the interview process when we are hiring. I monitor reactions: how the person reacts to what's being said and whether or not they truly are willing to learn. We look for attributes related to attitude and behaviour. The messages are always consistent: first, "it's OK to make a mistake – but learn from it" and second, "whilst we don't expect absolute perfection, we expect people to try to be perfect – there is a difference". If that's not for them, and they're not willing to be pushed every day to deliver perfection and gain satisfaction from it, then this is not the right field, by no means the right fit.

What separates very good from great? A front of house presence is critical. All guests want to be recognised to varying degrees. This does require the collective effort of the whole team; driving and developing relationships is the basis of what we do. There is no time for egos in this business; egos must be left at home. Our guests, however, reserve the right to have great self-appreciation; we should accommodate this. I often think that studies in psychology would serve hoteliers well.

Often those who complete degrees or programmes in hotel schools or universities expect to take on senior roles quickly. It's easy for me to say, "Remain patient". With this, I mean one shouldn't underestimate the value of working in a team, the value of working at the grassroots, understanding why things in a hotel are done the way they are done. Question always what you are doing and why. Don't turn on the blinkers and become robotic.

People with the correct attitude – a 'can do' attitude – who are humble and willing to sacrifice from time to time and take the good with the bad have every chance of doing well. These colleagues will naturally stand out and hence the chances of succeeding are far greater. A sense of pride in what one does also plays an enormous role in spotting the colleagues who can go to the next level.

I have thoroughly enjoyed every moment of my career thus far. Each day is different and I never cease to be amazed by what I am fortunate enough to witness. I also feel blessed to have met so many outstanding individuals both as colleagues and guests. Thankfully, my passion for pleasing guests remains until today and therefore 'working' is a privilege.

LUC DELAFOSSE

Hôtel de Crillon, Paris

Hôtel de Paris, Monaco

The Imperial Hotel, Torquay

The Savoy Hotel, London

The Vista Palace Hotel, Roquebrune-Cap-Martin

Le Grand Hôtel, Le Touquet Paris-Plage

Hôtel Mirabeau, Monaco

The Ritz Hotel, London

Hotel Burj Al Arab, Dubai

Hôtel de Crillon, Paris

Waldorf Astoria, Beverly Hills

Always say "Yes".

I had a very nice childhood, a very simple quiet life. We lived very close to the hub of Paris, in Hauts-de-Seine to be exact. My family had a little packaging industry, a family company in the suburbs of Paris. My father worked with his brothers; he was the accountant. My mother was a secretary.

I was not really meant to embrace the hospitality industry but I was not able to enter the army as I wanted to do originally and therefore Plan B was that I would try hotel school. At the time, my elder brother was in Jura at another school, so for convenience my parents said, "OK, since you missed your entry to the army, and you want to look at going to a hotel school, you should consider Poligny because your brother is nearby". So when I was about 15 years old, I went to the *École Hotelier de Poligny* in Jura, a nice hotel school that is doing very well today, and I ended up being there for three years.

I loved hotel school. It was the first time that I was away from my family, away from Paris, and I still have a lot of friends from those days from 1978. That's where, for example, I met my wife! She's still my wife, my dear wife, today! And we both have a lot of friends from our days in that school. So those good times are still very much present in my memory and in my mind today.

And that's when and where it all started for me in the hospitality industry. I wanted to work alongside my studies so I used to work in a lot of small restaurants, hotel restaurants, in the whole of Jura. I remember, for example, working in Poligny, in Dijon, and at the *Chevaliers de Tastevin* events in Beaune. I started as a chef at the same time as attending hotel school, in a hotel in a very small village called Bonlieu in Jura. It's a very interesting link in my whole career. The name of the hotel was Hôtel Auberge de la Poutre – it is still open today for the season – and the name of the owner, the chef / owner, was M. Denis Moureaux. For me, this was where it all started.

Although I was working as a chef, sometimes I waited on tables as well if there were too many guests – I did a little bit of everything in that small hotel. I worked at the weekends, during the holidays and so on. In fact, I worked for three years on and off and when I finished up at school, I did the 'season', the summer season.

During that time, there was a family on holiday in that small village from Monaco, Monte Carlo. The old man – he was old to me at that time, I was very young, maybe 19 – used to come every day to have his coffee at the bar with his newspaper and then two or three days in the week he used to come for lunch or dinner. By the end of the summer, he was good friends with M. Moureaux and he said, "This young man (meaning me), he is fantastic. You should do something with him. You should send him somewhere where he could learn and make some progress". The old man – his name was M. Accatino – had been the restaurant manager until 1945 of the Empire Room at the Hôtel de Paris in Monaco, Monte Carlo. So my boss said, "M. Accatino, if you say so, why don't you do something for him? Because he needs to go at the end of the season". And M. Accatino said, "OK". I still remember seeing him picking up the telephone, calling Monaco, Monte Carlo from Bonlieu, and asking to speak to M. Pastor.

"M. Pastor, how are you? I am on holidays in Jura. I have a fantastic young man for you. Do you think you can employ him as a *commis* waiter? In September? OK, OK, yes, good, I'll speak to you later. Thank you very much". And he looked at my boss and at me and said, "Done!".

So after the season ended, I arrived in Monaco, Monte Carlo. I had the name of the manager and the name of the hotel: M. Pastor, Hôtel de Paris. I was 20 years old. I took a taxi from the station to the hotel and I was so afraid getting out of the taxi with my suitcase. I said, "I am here to see M. Pastor" and so they sent me to the office and there I met M. Pastor. "Ah, here is the young man coming from M. Accatino". He called somebody else and said, "Please, take care of him" and that was how I started as a *commis* waiter at the Hôtel de Paris, in Monaco, Monte Carlo.

In those days, you had to start at the lower levels in the industry. There was a fantastic brigade at the Hôtel de Paris, a brigade of 50 people – *commis* waiters, *chefs de rang*, headwaiters and managers – between the Empire Room and the Grill on the eighth floor. I started as a wine *commis*, and then I moved onto *commis de suite*. As a *commis* waiter, you assist your *chef de rang* to bring all the dishes from the kitchen to the waiter-station but you are not allowed to go near the table with the guests at that stage still: you have to learn. Then I learnt to be a *commis de tranche* – that's when you learn all the skills of carving: *flambée* and so on. If you were a good *commis*, after one or two years you could become a *chef de rang* and for all the *commis* as I was that the prime objective – your white bow tie would change to a *black* bow tie to signify your promotion! But in most cases, people were promoted to *chef de rang* only after maybe five, six or seven years of being a *commis*. That was the old days – some people would argue against the system but for me it was the very good old days. I spent almost two years at the Hôtel de Paris, leaving only because I had to do my military service, back in Paris.

What I had learnt, working in a brigade like that, were very strong values: of hard work, of friendship, of engagement, of *parole*, when you give your word to your colleagues. A brigade is like a family – and what I loved was that in the brigade you had the youngsters like us *commis* waiters in their 20s and you also had head waiters in their 50s, 60s even. It was a great family. I also learnt, that to have a successful career in the hotel industry, it was important to speak English – at the time, the Hôtel de Paris was sending people to London, to fantastic hotels like The Savoy and The Dorchester. I decided that when I completed my military service, I would go to London to work and to learn English.

So I went back to Paris and did my military service. Again an extraordinary experience, because when I did the process of application for where you will be positioned during your year of military service, I was asked, "What do you do?", so I said, "I am a waiter, I am a *chef de rang*". "OK, where did you work?" "At the Hôtel de Paris, Monaco, Monte Carlo." So they said, "OK, we will give you a choice" – in fact, I had three choices! Here in Paris, they gave me the choice to transfer, first, to the Defence Minister, second, to the Minister for Labour and Work, and third, to the *Assemblée Nationale*. So I said "I'll take the *Assemblée*". So I went to the *Assemblée Nationale,* under the impression that I was to take over the head waiter position. But when I arrived at the *Assemblée Nationale*, they said, "Oh, you are the one who is taking over from the head chef". I didn't say anything. I thought I'd see how it worked out. So I ended up taking over from the head chef for one day and a half.

The first evening, I did an official cocktail party and dinner party for 45 people. At the end of the dinner, the President of the *Assemblée Nationale* arrived in the kitchen and said, "You are the new chef!". I said, "Yes, President". "Are you happy here?" "Yes, I am very happy here." He said, "OK, so tell me what you have done so far" and so I explained to him what I did. "OK, so you haven't cooked for some time?" I said, "Yes, for quite some time, I have been a waiter at the Hôtel de Paris, in Monaco, Monte Carlo" and he said, "Yes, I could see that". That I will always remember! And then he said, "Fantastic, you did very well. But tomorrow you will go back where you came from and we will see what they will do with you".

So I went back to the transfer centre in Paris the next day and I said, "It didn't work out because I think they were expecting a professional chef". So they said, "No problem, we have had to transfer the head waiter who was sent to the Defence Minister, so you will go to the Defence Ministry straightaway". So I went to the Ministry. In those days – this was 1982 – the Minister was Charles Hernu, and the President of France was François Mitterand. So I spent a year and a month there at the Defence Ministry and I have to say that was sensational. What made it so good was that I saw so many heads of state, coming to the Defence Ministry, attending official dinners, official cocktails, official meetings, and I learnt so much. It was wonderful to have this opportunity to learn certain aspects of what we would call today the work of a butler. Effectively, I was the private butler for the Defence Minister for a year – at home, when he was actually in Paris. When he used to travel, someone else travelled with him – and because he used to travel quite a bit, I had free time to work in hotels as a casual waiter or head waiter. I still planned after military service to go to London – and that's how I found myself in London in December 1983.

I started in London as a *chef de rang* in a French restaurant in Hampstead, called Keats Restaurant. The owner, M. Aron Misan, was a great boss, and I still recall having news from him up until two years ago. The whole team – kitchen and service – was actually French except the chef. The chef was British, in a French restaurant! I got on very well with my colleagues, I made good friends there. My wife, Sylvie, who was not yet my wife at the time, I had met her at hotel school, was with me. She was working in another restaurant in London.

After a few months, we decided to move to Torquay. I worked in The Imperial in Torquay; my wife worked in another hotel. We liked living in Torquay. At that time, Sylvie and I found that our English was not improving as much or as fast as we wanted, so I looked around Torquay and found the South Devon College, which had a training programme for the Hotel Catering International Management Association (HCIMA), now the Institute of Hospitality. I joined South Devon College for HCIMA Part A – I think I worked six days and went to school on the seventh! It was a little bit of a repetition of what I had learnt in the hotel school but still it was very good because it was in English. It was a fantastic time: I was working, I was learning English, and I was learning my job as well.

I think my desire to learn came from my family – they were extremely hardworking, I have to say perhaps even too much. The fact that you can learn and grow very quickly is particularly important in the hospitality or hotel industry because it's true that if you work hard you can actually make it. There is no substitute for hard work. I have done it enough to believe it. From the day I joined hotel school, I was not subsidised by my family. I was on my own, and it was sometimes extremely tough. But, I had two days off, and there were always hotels or restaurants that wanted me to work extra casual time as a chef or as a waiter. So you work and in the end you get paid and you have money to spend during the week! I understood that and was willing to do it, so it was quite simple to enjoy life.

Then after a year and a half, Sylvie (now my fiancée) and I decided to go back to London and we thought, "We have to do something better than we have done up to now" so we joined The Savoy, in 1984. It was – still is – an outstanding hotel, an institution, a worldwide institution. There was one General Manager during my four years at The Savoy whom I know today and still look up to today: Willy Bauer. The Savoy gave me the opportunity to continue my studies so I joined Ealing College, which is now part of the University of West London, where I completed my HCIMA. At The Savoy, I worked in the bar, in the restaurants and in the back of house. I finished my four years at The Savoy as the Back of House Manager. The Back of House Manager's department at The Savoy was perhaps one of the hardest departments to work in – but that's how you can learn a lot. There were about 50 to 60 stewards, people working in washing-up areas, banqueting set-up and so on, cleaning furniture in the back of house. I had to use a lot of psychology to get people to work well together. Human relationships play a very important part in success as a team and I really learnt a lot about management skills, in particular how to deal with people both individually and as a team. The Savoy in those days was like a family and I made a lot of friends. I actually employed some of them later on in my career and still see them today.

In London, my wife and I lived first near Hampstead, in a lovely area called Chalk Farm. I remember a discothèque there where we used to go, and also a tea and coffee shop. We were among a bunch of French people who were not making a lot of money but enjoying a good life. Then we moved to Camberwell, near Elephant & Castle. In 1987, we decided to go back to France and get married. So I suggested, "Why don't we try to go back to Monaco and see whether we can find a job there?". We took a few days off and went back to Monaco. I had written to a few general managers of hotels there and the General Manager of the Hôtel de Paris agreed to meet me. He said, "Your resumé is good. You have done very well up to now. You are now Chief Steward of The Savoy – fantastic. But what do you want to do?". I told him, "I want to become Food & Beverage Manager. That's my objective". He said, "Unfortunately, I don't have any vacancies but I am interested in you. If you agree, I will recruit you as a Chief Steward in six months' time, on the promise that, if there is a change in the food and beverage department, you will be the first to get the job". So I said, "That's interesting". I said to my wife, "We want to go back to France. We want to get married. I have an opportunity in Monaco six months from now, so why don't we try?". So we decided to go back to France in the next six months.

I actually resigned from The Savoy to take the opportunity of joining Le Meridien for six months. The Meridien group had taken over The Piccadilly Hotel in London, and renamed it Le Meridien Piccadilly, and they were looking for young managers to create a task force for managing the change. I don't remember how exactly I had the contact but I found myself telling them, "In about six months, I will be going back to France to join the Hôtel de Paris in Monaco, Monte Carlo, but I would be happy to participate in this project to implement and deploy all the Standard Operating Procedures within the hotel". So I started in the rooms division, and spent six months setting up procedures, working in the daytime or night-time, answering to the head of the rooms division and the number two of the hotel, and deploying systems and procedures. It was like a crash course: the rooms division was something that I didn't know very well up till then.

I then realised that, by making some quick leaps instead of ordinary steps early in your career, you can learn a lot more. I would say that, if you can manage in the first 10 years of your career to learn as much as you can about technical skills of the hotel industry, you prepare yourself for a very good management career after that.

❖

Sylvie and I got married in June 1987. I was Chief Steward in the Hôtel de Paris and she worked in those days in a bigger hotel, The Loews, in Monaco. I knew already most of the people in the food and beverage department in the Hôtel de Paris because I had been a *commis* waiter there. It was like going back home, back to my professional family. And, to me, the Hôtel de Paris has never had since then so good a time in the food and beverage department with a very admirable team spirit.

Six months later, the Executive Assistant Manager (EAM) in charge of food and beverage, number three of the hotel's managers, left. I had a promise. I had a promise! Wasn't it fantastic? After a little while, yes, the position was offered to me, so I became EAM F&B at the Hôtel de Paris in 1987. I was 25.

A few months later, the General Manager, Karl Vanis, one of my mentors, left to join another hotel just outside Monaco, called today The Vista Palace Hotel. He said to me, "Come with me. If you agree, you will become my number two and we will re-open this jewel of a hotel together". Can you guess what decision I made? Did I say "Yes" or did I say "No"? Of course, I said, "Yes". Because all the 'Yes' decisions I had made up to now had been good decisions for me, I said I would continue on that path. I had learnt that, when there is an opportunity for you to improve, progress or gain a new experience, you always have the choice of saying "No" or you have the choice of saying "Yes". If you say "Yes" and put your values of engagement, hard work and willingness into it, there is no reason to fail.

So I chose to follow my mentor as number two and became Hotel Manager of The Vista Palace Hotel in 1988. We re-opened the hotel together and this was a very important 'leap' in my career because it was the first time that I had the opportunity to work at a senior management level in a hotel that was closed for reconstruction and to re-open it. I was faced with construction issues, preparing for the re-opening, under the leadership of somebody I knew, somebody I trusted and who trusted me. I had three remarkable years – they went like three months. I loved it all.

We had been open for about two years and guess what happened? One day, a Saturday, while I was on duty, a visitor came in and asked reception, "I would like to see around your hotel". So I met the gentleman – he was an Egyptian gentleman. While I was showing him around the hotel, he asked me more and more questions, "How long have you been open? How did you do it? Were you here? Did you supervise the construction?" and many more. After about an hour and a half of this 'interviewing' visit, he said, "Goodbye, it was very enjoyable. Thank you very much. I may contact you again". Three weeks later, he called me, "M. Delafosse, I am M. XX (I will not mention his name), do you remember me? You so kindly showed me your hotel and I was wondering whether you could come and visit me in my house in Juan-les-Pins. I would like to discuss some business matters with you". Not too shy any more, I said, "Yes, of course, with pleasure".

I went out there that evening and he showed me the plans of a new hotel property in Le Touquet Paris-Plage, situated at the opposite end of France from the Principality of Monaco, where he and a British partner had decided to build The Grand Hôtel Le Touquet. He said, "Luc, you really impressed me. I want you to be our General Manager to build and open this five star hotel for us". I had spent about three years at The Vista Palace, it was a good opportunity for me, it would be my first General Manager position and a fantastic opportunity as well because it was a new project. So I said, "Yes".

In 1991, my wife and I arrived in Le Touquet. After a few months we opened this 'first class' hotel. Even today, I consider the Le Touquet experience as my best life experience. I wouldn't say necessarily the best hotel experience, but my best life experience because our two daughters, Emilie and Charlotte, were born in Le Touquet. I had a fantastic hotel, I had a fantastic team, it was my first General Manager position and again I learnt so much ...

One day, out of the blue, I received a call from my mentor, Karl Vanis at the Vista Palace Hotel in Monaco, Monte Carlo. He said, "Luc, I am calling you because there is an opportunity that I wouldn't like you to miss". I said, "Why is it too good to miss?". He said, "Surely you are not going to stay in Le Touquet? Surely you are going to come back to Monaco?".

"Maybe. Why? I am quite happy here. It's a lovely area and I love it but I'm three years here now". "It's for a small hotel, part of the Société des Bains de Mer de Monaco (SBM), called the Hôtel Mirabeau." "Yes, of course, I know it." "Do you know the owners? Because that hotel has a particularity: although it is operated by the SBM, it is privately owned. It is the only hotel within the SBM group in Monaco that is not owned by the State Principality. It is privately owned by some very nice gentlemen, regular guests of the Hôtel de Paris. I mentioned your name, they didn't remember you but I am sure that, when they see you and you see them, they will remember and the link will be recreated." I said, "Fantastic, of course I will come back to Monaco for interview". I went for the interview and was offered the General Manager's position at the Hôtel Mirabeau, managed by the SBM, under private ownership. So in January 1993, we moved back with our two daughters to Monaco and I re-joined the SBM for the third time as General Manager of the Hôtel Mirabeau.

I used to meet with the owners of The Mirabeau from time to time. They were very nice and, clearly, the best people I have ever worked for in my whole career – and I say this on purpose because it is true. One day in late 1994, I was told: "In a few weeks' time, you will hear fantastic news. It's like a childhood dream come true". Two or three weeks later, I read in the press that my owners had just bought The Ritz in London!

In January 1995, during a discussion with over coffee, I asked how things were going with the Ritz. The reply was that there were a few challenges here and there and they were still trying to understand the hotel, the building, the organisation, etc. I was quite 'curious' about it and, just as a matter of courtesy and politeness, said: "You know, if there is anything I can do, I'd be very happy to help". "OK, thank you, thank you", that was it. A week later, I had my monthly meeting on the renovation that we were doing at The Mirabeau. Usually this was with the owner's representative but this time it was with one of the owners. He asked me, "Luc, do you remember the conversation last week?". Honestly, I could not remember but he actually pointed at me and said, "Didn't you say that you could help at the Ritz?". "Yes, of course, I remember". As I said that, he looked at me and said, "Luc, you start next week".

I went home that evening and told my wife, "I may have to go back to London next week – to work at The Ritz". "What are you going to do?" "I don't know." I arrived at 11pm on a Sunday night at The Ritz, I was given a key and went to my room. The following morning at 8am I went down and sat in the Palm Court of The Ritz and ordered coffee. About 8.30 or 8.45, I saw a gentleman in a morning coat walking down the long gallery from the restaurant and then I saw the same gentleman walking back quite fast! As I was the only person in the Palm Court at the time, he looked at me, stopped, came up to me and said, "Are you Mr. Delafosse?". I said, "Yes, I am". "I am Tom O'Connell, the General Manager of The Ritz, and I was told to meet you here this morning. Someone will come from head office this morning and tell us what exactly you will be doing here – as we will work together".

On that day, I was given the brief to implement a blitz cleaning of the hotel over a period of four to five months. So we made a plan: taking a room out of order for a day, a suite for two days, changing whatever needed to be changed, bedding, carpets, curtains, etc. – repainting the room, deep cleaning the bathroom, changing all the equipment that needed to be changed and so on, fixing the furniture, checking electrical and air-conditioning and bringing the room back into use on the following day. We completed the 130 rooms according to the plan within five months. I was going back to Monaco to see my family once or twice every month and to oversee the Hôtel Mirabeau of course, where I was still General Manager with all my responsibilities.

In May every year, there is the Grand Prix de Monaco, so I had to be back for that major event. During that week, I was asked to consider moving back to London at the end of the summer season to continue on the plan and to take on the responsibility of managing The Ritz in London as General Manager. I was told, "It will all be done correctly, keeping the hotel open". I had become good friends with Tom O'Connell by that time and he told me that he was going back to Dublin, "My family is in the restaurant life in Dublin so I will open a restaurant, a *brasserie*" – this was O'Connell's restaurant, now in Donnybrook. Tom had been the General Manager of The Ritz under the ownership of Trafalgar House Group and Food & Beverage Manager at The Savoy before moving to The Ritz. I'd like to salute him because he was, and still is, a great hotelier. After having found a replacement for the Hôtel Mirabeau, I re-joined The Ritz London in September 1996.

When I look back, I realise that the past is important because, if you want to think of a bright future, you have to build it on a strong past. And you only create your past and your future in the present. I would never have been able to work on three separate occasions in Monaco if my present situations, at the time, had not given me that opportunity. I would never have been able to become General Manager at The Ritz in London if my present at the Hôtel Mirabeau and at the Hôtel de Paris, before that, had not given me the chance. But it's all in our hands – here and now – and to me this is the testimony that, if you want a career in the hospitality business, this is how you create opportunities without knowing it.

The period between 1996 and 2003 were very interesting years at The Ritz. The decision was made to keep the hotel open while managing a massive refurbishment programme. The owners invested a lot of money during the first four or five years between 1996 and 2000 – all the rooms, public areas and the kitchens were completed renovated. It was more like a restoration process than a renovation process.

At that point, I realised that you have to make the conscious decision in your career between either moving every two and a half years or when you take on a job and give your word, you must fulfil the promise. To me, this is very important. When I take on a role, I don't take it for two years and then I will see; I engage myself as if I planned to stay there forever. When I look at someone's resumé and I see that the person is more a 'collector' of names, titles and hotels, I am always very sceptical about the commitment and values of that particular person – and in general I turn out to be right.

After almost eight years at The Ritz, London, one day I received a call and was asked if I would consider perhaps going to Dubai, living and working there, to take on the role of the General Manager of the most luxurious hotel in the world: The Hotel Burj Al Arab. I think that why they were interested in me was my eight years at The Ritz and my time at The Savoy and The Hôtel de Paris before that – surely mainly my eight years at The Ritz London. I met two great hoteliers and gentlemen, Gerald Lawless, now Vice Chairman of the Jumeirah Group, and Guy Crawford, COO of the group. I remember, clearly, Gerald telling me, "Luc, you and I, we must not fail. You will be the fourth General Manager in the first four years of The Hotel Burj Al Arab since it opened. We need now to give The Burj Al Arab some stability and I rely on you to reposition the hotel and to bring it to excellence where it should be". I said, "Fine, I have the brief".

I stayed almost five years in Dubai – so I fulfilled my promise again. I had a marvellous time and was pleased with the decision to move on from The Ritz in London to Dubai because it was a completely different experience, professionally and personally for me and for my family. I didn't decide to leave The Ritz to move next door, I decided to leave for a different life experience – joining a group rather than an independent hotel, in a brand new hotel. Only four years old, The Burj Al Arab was a unique and exceptional hotel. These were good reasons for me to move on.

Personally I think that the vision for Dubai is a great message for, and to, the world. It's saying that we are here to create something for people; come to Dubai, you will see it and you will live it – that's what I have done for five years and I am very proud to have played been a tiny part in that very special adventure. In five years in Dubai, I learnt a great deal, achieved a lot and above all, met some fantastic people – colleagues and guests. There was not one day without a celebrity, head of state or somebody famous in the hotel. What I will always remember most from my time at The Burj Al Arab is that, as General Manager, you are engaged in the daily operation of your hotel, working with your colleagues or associates, for the guests. When you exchange and give to people, people will immediately give back to you – good or bad!

Then after almost five years in Dubai, it was time for my daughters to think about going away to university, perhaps back to a city in Europe. And so I was starting to have, let's be honest, a bit of a dilemma, whether I stay in Dubai or whether I make the conscious decision to go back to Europe and take care of my family.

Very soon, an opportunity of going back to London arose. I made the acquaintance of some private investors originally from Russia, who had a first class hotel project in London, the Poultry project. Right outside Bank Tube station, in the City of London, there is the Midland Bank building, designed originally by the architect Edwin Lutyens. The project was to renovate the building and convert it into a five star deluxe hotel. Again, I was able to engage with great people and owners; I had a fantastic time working with them. But unfortunately, the financial crisis hit in 2009 and the project was postponed.

The decision to leave because of the uncertainty of the project gave me an opportunity in Paris, my home town, to join the Hôtel de Crillon in January 2010. I was recruited by the ownership company Starwood Capital (not the same as Starwood Hotels), whose CEO was Barry Sternlitch, which had bought the hotel from the Taittinger Group in 2006. The plan, initially, was to refurbish it to its former glamour – in the end, the Hôtel de Crillon was sold to a private investor in 2011. The new owner quickly decided on a complete renovation of the hotel. So after the sale, I was entrusted with the process of closing the hotel in March 2013 and starting an extraordinary process of re-construction and renovation. In 2014, it came under a new management company, Rosewood Hotels & Resorts – and that's where I was until mid-2015, two years after, preparing for the opening of this iconic hotel in Paris.

Looking back, I realise that one of the skills that a leader should master is decision-making. Decisiveness is key in the life of a leader – particularly in the hotel industry because you are making decisions about a lot of different things on a daily basis, 24/7, and as the General Manager you are seen as the person to always make the right decision.

A GM needs to be able to do three things. One is to master conversations, whether they be with colleagues, guests, people from the trade, and so on – a GM should be able to engage with people in a positive manner in every situation on every subject. The second is decision-making. These two skills come with one more: the willingness to listen always and be a good listener.

In my case, I was very fortunate to become a GM very young and I can say that I have learnt the skills of being a GM on the job. Also I can happily say today that I am a better GM than when I started!

With all I have done in the last 30 years, there are perhaps some lessons that may be useful for the younger generation. I have shared what happened in my career and life but I also went through a lot of peaks and troughs at work and in my private life. I have to say that what has always won in all those situations – particularly the difficult situations and I have had a 'fair share' of those – was that I have never lost motivation and positiveness. What often helped me was to focus on what I had achieved in the past; this solid base helped me to believe that, if I continued the way I had done until then, I might not necessarily win but surely I would not fail!

I learnt one thing that is quite important: whenever you stop before a difficulty because you find it too difficult, that's where you fail; however, if you work through that difficulty, whatever the outcome, that's when you win! I can use the words of Sir Winston Churchill – they are as valid now as they were 50 years ago – "Never give in. Except to convictions of honour and good sense".

If you want to manage a hotel or any business, you set objectives. But be careful that, in setting objectives, you are not perhaps limiting yourself to a level that you could 'easily' exceed. If you are prepared to give everything you have, if you have no limits, if you don't set limits for yourself, you will exceed what you thought you could achieve – definitely! It's very simple, and I have never been shy in my career about giving myself in work, in people, in commitments, and particularly when an opportunity arises because that's when it is 'crucial' to demonstrate your determination.

To me, the characteristics of a good hotelier today are first having the right personality and skills for the job – it's very clear that's the basics. Second, you must develop some talent for people, with people, and this skill probably needs to be constantly appraised and improved on. This is where feedback comes into play and is critical to any development of one's personality or skills.

Also, as hotels go with travel, a polished hotelier must be a good traveller. This is quite easy today and it could help a lot or save you from embarrassing situations when you welcome and look after guests coming from all over the world. A good hotelier must know his customers well and understand the different cultures and customs from diverse backgrounds – understanding that certain things are not necessarily seen as the same, depending on whether you are in Asia, or in the Middle East or in the Western World is essential in managing an international hotel.

There is another important skill in adapting to each and every guest depending on the situation and circumstances. The job is in a way all to do with communicating the key message: "As General Manager of this hotel, I am at your service. Please do not hesitate to call upon me, I will be very pleased to serve you". This is as simple as it is effective at the same time – but it has to come from the top.

Sadly, too many general managers feel that they are somehow above their guests as well as above their employees. No, we are at their service – always. Service is therefore the skill to be reinvented over and over again. Of course, it can be taught and developed – I didn't know as much before as I know today. Personally, I am always on the look-out to take part in the service aspect, on the 'floor' as we say. I am happy to wait on a guest and to make sure that he or she is satisfied with our service. I am not shy of the word 'important'; we are here to make our customers feel important while they are visiting our hotels. We are here to make them feel like kings – yes, this is our job to make each guest feel that he is king of the castle!

At The Burj Al Arab, I managed a team of almost 2,000 colleagues and employees and, for all employees, this is a strong message when you actually do what you say, when you demonstrate that you are capable of welcoming a guest, of waiting on a guest or even serving a glass of water because it is 'important'. Like many hoteliers, I enjoy spending time in the lobby for an hour at certain times of the day to speak with guests and employees. This alone is our duty! Some GMs would say, "Oh, I have a number two to do this or I have other more important matters to deal with". But this is a great way to gain feedback and be approachable. However, one can perhaps miss out on other things, on other aspects of the job, so it is important to know what to do, when to do it and how to do it in order to be more effective.

Another aspect of the job that, I think, hoteliers can demonstrate is warmth, empathy and even affection. I had to develop this part of my personality and over the years I am glad to say that my efforts have paid back. Peter Burwash, a highly sought-after international speaker, said that he has never seen a GM with so much empathy – this is one of the greatest compliments I have received. Empathy can be developed – if you learn the skill to adapt to guests, showing empathy whenever necessary and appropriate, this can be critical to the success or failure of one's leadership style.

What about passion? I know I come across as very passionate about my work, I just love it! To the point that some people think, "Perhaps he is overdoing it". I like to show passion, and I like to show it because it can also motivate employees and please guests.

In Dubai for example, the airport is open 24 hours, with planes taking off and landing at night. For any of the luxury hotels in Dubai, it would be acceptable for the General Manager to introduce himself to certain VIP guests the day after they arrived, and check then that everything is fine. That might be acceptable in any hotel in Dubai – but to make it The Burj Al Arab, I made the decision to be there at the front door to welcome each and every VIP – over and over again, as regularly as possible. It could be exhausting and truly sometimes I felt worn out! But I can assure you the smile on the face of the guests when the General Manager of The Hotel Burj Al Arab was in the lobby or just outside the door to welcome them in the early hours of the morning was well worth the effort. I then just needed a little follow-up during the stay and to be present at their departure. In this way, you set high standards for your team. Another most efficient habit was my daily visits of the restaurants at breakfast, lunch and dinner times.

Also, I used to enjoy – that's the correct word – going to the guest floors and meeting colleagues and guests (unhappy guests). The objective was to meet new guests and make new friends. I liked doing it – to the point that sometimes I had to warn myself because my PA used to call me, "Luc, where are you? So-and-so is waiting for you now". There was a great sense of satisfaction after a long day's work when you have met some guests, happy or not necessarily happy, and feel that you have accomplished your job of host properly.

The hotel business is known for long working hours and the challenge or difficulty is to manage our private life – so if you talk with my wife about this perhaps she will have a different view, but I can honestly say that these little tips helped me in doing my job for years and I loved it all.

The general manager's job has evolved and changed. It has become much more strategic than it used to be. It used to be extremely operational and it has now become much more strategic. I think it's only fair that a GM knows about operations – the base is operations. The GM needs to know what the executive chef is supposed to do, how the waiters are supposed to be waiting on guests, how a housekeeper is supposed to clean a room, how an accountant is supposed to do his job as well, how a sales manager is supposed to set his activities. All these functions are very important but, in addition, the focus has become much more on strategy – and it also has become much more 'social' orientated, requiring interpersonal skills with guests and employees. And in order to do that, you need to be on the floor more than ever.

What increases the gap between hotels today is first that a hotel is the *vitrine* of life – and not only a place to 'sleep'. It is the small front window of life that needs to be invented or re-invented for guests day in and day out. In any hotel, guests and employees interact together; in a deluxe hotel, that interaction should be based on luxury and quality and excellence in everything we do from the arrival to the departure and even beyond. All good hotels actually deliver more or less the same 'experience', and probably in the much same manner, so what differentiates an exceptional hotel from another 'normal' luxury hotel? It is, for me, that the exceptional hotel reflects the place of its location, its style and its promise. We hoteliers today need to challenge any *status quo*. We need to create an edge and always be trying to reinvent it.

The other aspect that can set a hotel apart from its competitors in its market is how the team, starting from the general manager, set the tone and play their part. We must always offer our guests a place to be able to relax and to feel secure. Particularly nowadays, everything must work extremely well with no glitches. Everybody must act in the right way so guests feel extremely comfortable and we must exceed their expectations – a good location, nice rooms and good food are not enough – we must include positive 'emotions' in our processes too!

This is not a simple task for a team to achieve over and over again because not everybody has the skill to smile each and every time he or she interacts with a guest; not everybody understands how to anticipate guest's needs which is better than to react, often too late; not everybody can actually dedicate enough time because of their many other priorities. But to me, it is crucial that, at each and every interaction, we make the time to have a proper conversation with the guest –

and with good manners. The time we spend with employees and guests must always be 'quality time'. The end result should meet their needs and lead to a positive outcome in order to surpass and exceed their expectations. Observing your hotel, listening to feedback and reacting fast are key. Nowadays, with improved technology, the Internet and social media help hoteliers in being more effective but 'direct interaction' is still critical.

If I could advise someone who wants to progress in the hotel industry, there would be a lot of things to explain, but let me take one or two things specifically. One, understand clearly the job and really put in the effort – even if you are very gifted and talented, you cannot achieve anything without putting in effort. Second, I think you have to be a good communicator. For example, in the five star 'Palace' hotels in Paris, up to 80% of the guests we welcome on a daily basis come from a foreign country, and do not necessarily speak French. At every level – housekeeper, receptionist, waiter, manager – we must make the effort to speak English, the international language. I would say this is a minimum to be able to communicate. If you understand, you can get feedback or make suggestions.

So I would always ask: "Do you have a passport? Do you speak English? Yes or no?". If you have a passport and can communicate, the world is yours. Today, the hotel industry offers so many different possibilities worldwide – and let's be honest, there are many more good hotels than there are good GMs so the job can be yours. The job is known to be 'tough' but it is not complicated. Serving a great product with a big smile on your face is not complicated!

When I was at The Burj Al Arab, I remember a head of state telling me, "Luc, what I would love is a good cup of tea". How would we serve a bad cup of tea at The Burj Al Arab? The real message behind his statement was that you can be very wealthy and live in luxury but sometimes you cannot get the most simple request served correctly. He was travelling on his private jet and asked for a 'cup of tea'. He was offered various flavours and said, "Can I get a normal cup of tea – English breakfast tea?". And unfortunately he couldn't get a good cup of tea on his own plane! I like the 'message' that there is no need to try to reinvent the art of service: keep it simple and to the point.

Also I like the fact that, in our business, you can interact – a GM and a head of state – with a guest and have a discussion about a 'good cup of tea'. That's what makes the job extremely interesting and rewarding – there are not many jobs where that can happen. The hotel business is unique in that way, that you can meet new people every day and you are offering simplicity and sophistication at the same time. If our job is to sell 'satisfaction', it is very important that we understand the mind-set of our guests and what they want. We also have to delight them, to offer them a little extra and that's where I feel that some functions are key in a five star hotel, such a concierge, a restaurant manager, the general housekeeper, executive chef and many more. We must add that little extra edge in our spirit of service in order to establish a creative relationship between the guest and an employee. In no trade is the relationship between so close and intimate as that between client and hotelier. First, we must gain the confidence of the guests – who may be in a bad mood, ready to find fault, wanting a fight – there are many hurdles to be cleared if he is

going to relax and enjoy the hotel and his food, and the first of
them is to like you.

I can tell you a story: at The Hotel Burj Al Arab, a head of state
from a small country was staying with us, and I was
summoned to his suite by his private secretary. When I
arrived, the secretary said, "I am busy with something. Can
you please wait?" so I had to wait in the lobby. After five
minutes or so, he came back and said, "Come with me" and I
followed him into the dressing room of the master bedroom of
the suite. The head of state was standing in the dressing room,
getting dressed for his next meeting. He started with
instructions for an event he wanted for the next day. The
private secretary took the jacket and went to hang it up. As he
had a bottle of perfume in his other hand and needed both
hands to hang the jacket, he gave me the bottle of perfume to

hold. Before he could take it back, the head of state gestured to
me to spray the perfume. And so I did. I sprayed the perfume
over him. Perhaps I am the only GM in this world to have
actually sprayed perfume on a head of state! I came out of that
suite thinking, "I love my job!".

I was very fortunate in my life that I have had a few great
mentors. My first mentor was my boss in a little village in Jura
where I worked in the kitchen and in service back in the late
1970s – M. Denis Moureaux. Afterwards, he came to visit me
in Monaco, he came to visit me in Le Touquet, he also came to
Dubai. Every year on my way to Switzerland to visit my
daughters, I stopped in the village of Bonlieu to present my
respects. This is important to me, going back to the roots of
where I started professionally.

A very special moment in my career was my first day as the General Manager at The Ritz in London. I was 35 years old and lived in Buckingham Gate. When I left home that morning, I walked through Green Park and St James' Park. Can you imagine, living in Buckingham Gate and working at The Ritz in London? What more did I want? And then entering the hotel, passing the concierge desk with the welcome from the hall porters …

Another special day was our arrival at The Hotel Burj Al Arab, in the escalator on my way up to the floors, my wife and my daughters with me. It meant a lot to me because I knew that my wife had made a great effort to make sure that things would go well for our daughters, her decision was critically 'important'. I would feel bad if I made a decision that was not what my wife would like us to do.

One of the greatest things in our industry is that you meet people who are very successful and important. Some I have met in almost all the hotels I was fortunate to manage. I remember meeting Mr. Bill Clinton at The Ritz many times, as well as Mrs. Hillary Clinton – I met them again at The Hotel Burj Al Arab on several occasions.

I was very fortunate, for example, to be part of the official visit of George W. Bush Jnr. to Dubai and to see the organisation and efforts made to welcome him as head of state – Dubai almost closed for that day. The meeting took place at The Hotel Burj Al Arab and it was nice to see my team in the picture taken with the President of the United States at that time. That is a great souvenir.

It was stunning to see Michael Jackson dancing around the fountain at The Burj Al Arab. On the way out of the hotel, at the top of the escalators, we passed near the fountain with the sequenced water display like a 'musical' show. Arriving at the fountain, Michael Jackson started to follow the tempo, snapping his fingers and suddenly started dancing around the fountain – unique! Special and fantastic!

At The Ritz in London, I felt very honoured as a French General Manager of The Ritz to be asked to organise the birthday party of Her Majesty the Queen in the main restaurant. I can say that Her Majesty the Queen spoke perfect French and spoke to me when I was accompanying her from the lobby of the hotel to the restaurant.

I have had guests who I met for the very first time at The Mirabeau in Monaco or at The Grand Hotel in Le Touquet, who visited me years after, in London at The Ritz and in Dubai at The Hotel Burj Al Arab. We had a lot of regulars at The Burj Al Arab, who continue to contact me today to make their reservations there! They say, "Luc, You know what I like. Please arrange the reservation for me".

The future for great hotels and great hoteliers is quite simple: it's all in service and emotional intelligence. Showing devotion and love, the relationship becomes more personal rather than impersonal. It's all about knowing what your guests want and gaining their confidence. Yes, we need to use technology and to master all the technical skills – but the future of our job is in human relationships. That's where the past comes from, where the present is happening and also where the future lies.

I can close with one simple word: Yes. Always say, "Yes". I know that in a lot of hotel companies you hear the motto "Never say 'No'". Myself, I would slightly change it to "Always say 'Yes'". It's positive, it's a commitment and much more: whenever there is an opportunity, it's "Yes"; whenever a guest wants me to do something, it's "Yes"; whenever an employee has a problem and wants me to help, it's "Yes". Always start with "Yes".

"Yes" can take you a long way.

INDEX

THE AUTHOR

Conor Kenny is the Founder and Principal of Conor Kenny & Associates, Ireland and the UK's leading independent training, mentoring, HR, learning and professional development company for the hospitality industry.

His skill is teaching and training the art of sales, marketing and business and growing talent. An advisor and mentor to several private and State companies, Conor is a columnist for the UK's hotel industry magazine. His view has been widely sought by the BBC (TV), Jools Holland (TV), BBC Scotland

(TV), BBC (Radio), Sky (TV), RTÉ (TV), RTÉ (Radio), NewsTalk (Radio), *USA Today*, *The Sunday Times*, *The Irish Times*, *The Sunday Business Post*, *The Irish Independent* and more. He is a syndicated writer for many global websites, including Cornell University and a regular contributor to business publications at home and abroad.

An expert communicator and strategist, Conor is a much in demand workshop facilitator where he guides businesses and people towards their strengths and is highly skilled at getting the best out of people.

His career started at Kilkenny Design and before Conor Kenny & Associates, he was Group Commercial Director for the Irish Pub Company, which designed and built Irish pubs in more than 70 countries. He has worked with many of the world's leading brands: Baileys, Guinness, Hennessy and Smirnoff, and international hotel groups and casino groups in Las Vegas have called on him.

In 2002 he founded Conor Kenny & Associates. Today, he and his team of specialists have over 200 Clients.

A passionate teacher and motivator, Conor is a frequent conference speaker, nationally and internationally, and has written key speeches for industry leaders.

Conor's years of experience are also employed to help advocate the charities he and his company work for.

Conor was educated at University College Dublin and the University of Greenwich, London.

A keen marathon runner, he also loves writing his award-winning blog. His first book, **SALES TALES: TRUE STORIES OF HOW GREAT SALES HAPPEN** was published by Oak Tree Press in 2014.

OAK TREE PRESS

Oak Tree Press develops and delivers information, advice and resources for entrepreneurs and managers. It is Ireland's leading business book publisher, with an unrivalled reputation for quality titles across business, management, HR, law, marketing and enterprise topics. NuBooks is its recently-launched imprint, publishing short, focused ebooks for busy entrepreneurs and managers.

In addition, Oak Tree Press occupies a unique position in start-up and small business support in Ireland through its standard-setting titles, as well training courses, mentoring and advisory services.

Oak Tree Press is comfortable across a range of communication media – print, web and training, focusing always on the effective communication of business information.

OAK TREE PRESS
E: info@oaktreepress.com
W: www.oaktreepress.com / www.SuccessStore.com.